edited with an introduction by Richard Willmott

# Four Metaphysical Poets

*An anthology of poetry by*
*Donne, Herbert, Marvell and Vaughan*

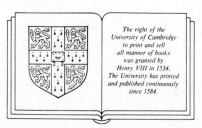

The right of the
University of Cambridge
to print and sell
all manner of books
was granted by
Henry VIII in 1534.
The University has printed
and published continuously
since 1584.

## Cambridge University Press

Cambridge
London   New York   New Rochelle
Melbourne   Sydney

Published by the Press Syndicate of the University of Cambridge
The Pitt Building, Trumpington Street, Cambridge CB2 1RP
32 East 57th Street, New York, NY 10022, USA
296 Beaconsfield Parade, Middle Park, Melbourne 3206, Australia

First published 1985

Printed in Great Britain at the University Press, Cambridge

Designed by Peter Holroyd
Cover by Paul Mountford

Library of Congress catalogue card number: 84-5800

*British Library cataloguing in publication data*
Four metaphysical poets.
1.English poetry—Early modern, 1500–1700
I.Willmott, Richard
821'.3'08   PR1205

ISBN 0 521 27758 2

# Contents

## Herbert

## Marvell

## Vaughan

## Other Poems

# Preface

The purpose of this anthology is to provide a sufficiently large selection of poetry by each of the four poets for an introductory study of them either individually or together. The fifth section is *not* intended as a further anthology of metaphysical poetry, indeed not all of it is metaphysical, but it provides background material for the purposes of comparison and elucidation.

In each section the love poems and religious poems have been separated. The love poems of Donne and the religious poems of Herbert and Vaughan have been arranged alphabetically for ease of reference, except that Vaughan's 'The Evening-Watch' follows 'The Morning-Watch'; there seemed no point in retaining the vestiges of the original order in which they were printed when so few of the poems would still have been next to their original neighbours. The poems of Marvell and those in the final section have been organised as far as possible according to theme.

The greatest need of the newcomer to metaphysical poetry is quite simply to understand the text and so I have given very full notes, but I have tried to avoid critical comments of a kind that might pre-empt the reader's judgement. I have quoted freely from the Bible, using the Authorised Version (1611), but I have used Miles Coverdale's translation of the Psalms from *The Book of Common Prayer* except where otherwise indicated.

The texts have been drawn from a variety of sources and have no authority. I have followed the emendation suggested by Edgar F. Daniels for line 72 of 'Regeneration' ('Vaughan's *Regeneration*: an emendation', *American Notes and Queries*, IX, 2 (1970), pp 19–20) and discussed by Alan Rudrum in his edition of Vaughan.

The spelling has been modernised except where to do so would unacceptably alter the sound of a word (e.g. *cutchannel* and *chymic*). I have made a sparing use of the apostrophe to show where words lose a syllable, but natural speech rhythms normally make clear where this happens and where words are elided. I have also indicated those places where the ending -tion is two syllables rather than one (-tiön) and where the final -ed should be pronounced (-èd).

The extent of my debt to others will immediately be apparent to anyone familiar with these poets. It would be impossible to list every obligation, but I should like in particular to acknowledge gratefully a debt to the editors listed under 'Further Reading' (and not only for those of their books listed there) and also to the work of Sir Herbert Grierson.

Richard Willmott
Brighton 1984

# Introduction

## Background

The poems in this anthology were written in a period of turbulent change and conflict. There were frequent outbreaks of war and civil war in Europe, and these were made all the more bitter by continual religious controversy. The overlapping of political and religious struggles is well illustrated by such episodes as the excommunication of Elizabeth I by the Pope in 1570 and the Gunpowder Plot against James I and VI in 1605. Because of the strength of their beliefs people were ready both to die and to kill for their religion. A long succession of such deaths, for example those of the Anglican bishops Cranmer and Ridley under the Roman Catholic Queen Mary, of the Jesuit poet Robert Southwell under the Anglican Elizabeth I, and Archbishop Laud under pressure from the Puritan party, culminated in the death of Charles I after the Civil War. That people were prepared to die reflected their view that the authorities which ordered their execution were, in Donne's words, not God's 'vicars [deputies], but hangmen to fate' and that to obey the state in matters of religion was 'idolatry' (Satire 3). Such an attitude provoked a strong response from most governments but, as Marvell pointed out, those who resort to force to impose their ideas can never relax their efforts:

The same arts that did gain
A power, must it maintain.
('An Horatian Ode', 119–20)

Nevertheless there were no further martyrs to religion after the restoration of Charles II, even though full religious toleration was still far away. Similarly foreign policy was no longer

influenced in the same way by religious sympathies – witness the
fact that whereas in 1596 Donne was taking part in Essex's
successful attack on Cadiz in which the fleet of Roman Catholic
Spain was destroyed, in 1667 Marvell was writing a satire on the
selfish incompetence that had led to a humiliating defeat at the
hands of a Protestant Dutch fleet that had sailed up the Medway
to attack Chatham:

> scratching courtiers undermine a realm,
> And through the palace's foundations bore,
> Burrowing themselves to hoard their guilty store.
> ('The Last Instructions to a Painter', 978–80)

Satire is not the literary form most frequently used by the
metaphysical poets, nor is it often thought of as being metaphysical, but it cannot be ignored. At the commencement of their
poetic careers Donne wrote, and Vaughan translated, satire,
while Marvell turned to it after he had finished with other forms
of verse. Donne and his contemporaries in the 1590s imitated
Roman satire, which Gilbert Highet describes as follows:

Satire is a continuous piece of verse, or of prose mingled with verse, of
considerable size, with great variety of style and subject, but generally
characterised by the free use of conversational language, the frequent
intrusion of its author's personality, its predilection for wit, humour,
and irony, great vividness and concreteness of description, shocking
obscenity in theme and language, an improvisatory tone, topical
subjects, and the general intention of improving society by exposing its
vices and follies. (*The Classical Tradition*)

The connection in style and content between satire of this type
and many of Donne's poems in particular is apparent.

In a poem about the expedition to the Azores to harry Spanish
shipping Donne typically questions his own motives as well as
those of others:

Whether a rotten state, and hope of gain,
Or, to disuse [free] me from the queasy pain
Of being beloved, and loving, or the thirst
Of honour, or fair death, out pushed me first,
I lose my end [purpose]: for here as well as I
A desperate may live, and a coward die.

('The Calm', 39–44)

This uneasiness about the underlying motives and morality of human behaviour appears again when Donne comments on man's self-destructive impulses, not least when through sexual immorality he runs the risk of the 'new disease', syphilis, which first appeared in Europe in the fifteenth century:

We seem ambitious, God's whole work to undo;
Of nothing he made us, and we strive too,
To bring ourselves to nothing back; and we
Do what we can, to do't as soon as he.
With new diseases on ourselves we war,
And with new physic [medicine], a worse engine far.

('An Anatomy of the World', 155–60)

Even Vaughan, the only one of the four poets in this anthology to play no part in public life, engages in satire. He writes about the 'darksome states-man' in an image which foreshadows Marvell's about the burrowing courtiers:

Yet digged the mole, and lest his ways be found
        Worked underground,
Where he did clutch his prey . . .

('The World' (1), 23–5)

The period was also one of new discoveries in such areas as anatomy, geography and astronomy. This last area was the most disturbing. The old ideas had combined the cosmography of Ptolemy (an Alexandrian astronomer and mathematician of the second century AD whose otherwise highly accurate calculations were based on the assumption that the earth was at the centre of the universe) with the theories of Greek philosophers such as Plato and Aristotle to put the earth at the centre of a spherical universe, the perfection of which had symbolised the harmony and order of God's creation (hence Galileo's trouble with the Roman Catholic Church when he challenged the old system):

We think the heavens enjoy their spherical,
Their round proportiön embracing all.
But yet their various and perplexèd course,
Observed in divers ages, doth enforce
Men to find out so many eccentric parts,

Such divers down-right lines, such overthwarts,
As disproportion that pure form.

('An Anatomy of the World', 251–7)

Indeed, as Donne puts it elsewhere in the same poem, the 'new philosophy calls all in doubt'.

Despite the development of these ideas about the universe older ways of thinking derived from the philosophy of Plato continued to be influential. Plato had taught that the physical universe of time and space was only a copy of a spiritual, ideal universe which is the true reality. This was an idea that could be easily assimilated to the Christian concept of an ideal heaven and an imperfect earth, as Vaughan does here:

I saw Eternity the other night
Like a great *Ring* of pure and endless light,
    All calm, as it was bright,
And round beneath it, Time in hours, days, years
        Driven by the spheres
Like a vast shadow moved, in which the world
    And all her train were hurled.

('The World' (1), 1–7)

Plato describes those who fail to see beyond this world to the ideal one as being like men in a cave with their backs to the entrance seeing only the shadows cast by a fire. They have no desire to be told that outside is the sun and the whole world. This idea also Vaughan adapts:

O fools (said I) thus to prefer dark night
        Before true light,
To live in grots, and caves, and hate the day
    Because it shows the way,
The way which from this dead and dark abode
        Leads up to God.

('The World' (1), 49–54)

Plato also suggested that men can be brought to love the ideal by ascending a 'ladder of love' which moves from the love of an individual to love of physical beauty, moral beauty, intellectual beauty and finally to love of the idea of beauty itself. This spiritualising effect of love is adapted by Donne:

If any, so by love refined,
    That he soul's language understood,
And by good love were grown all mind.

('The Ecstasy', 21–3)

The concept was combined in the Renaissance with that of courtly love to produce the theory of 'platonic love', a sexless union of minds such as Habington praises in his poems to Castara, but which many poets took pleasure in mocking. A typically humorous use of platonism occurs when Donne brushes aside the fact that he has had other mistresses before by suggesting that they were unreal, mere copies of his present mistress's ideal beauty:

    If ever any beauty I did see,
Which I desired, and got, 'twas but a dream of thee.

('The Good Morrow', 6–7)

The division between an ideal heaven and an actual earth leads to the theory that the soul (the ideal, real part of man) comes from heaven and yearns to return there, since on earth it can only see 'shadows of eternity' (Vaughan, 'The Retreat'). Similarly Marvell talks in 'The Garden' of the soul retreating into its own internal world, and in 'A Dialogue between the Soul and Body' shows the antipathy between a soul which longs for the spiritual reality of heaven and a body which is tied to this world.

Most importantly platonism provided a view of the universe in which all the parts were related and ordered (symbolised by the harmony of the music of the spheres as they revolved around the earth). Donne's lovers in 'The Sun Rising' can be a microcosm, a miniature copy of the world outside; Vaughan's lovers in 'To Amoret, of the Difference' are united by the same force that draws the compass to the north and keeps the planets in their places. It is a view which encourages that development of analogies (that exploration of the significant way in which certain objects share similar qualities and circumstances) which is crucial to metaphysical style.

The artistic developments of the period are also important to an understanding of metaphysical poetry. The tradition of setting lyric poetry to music, exemplified by composers such as Dowland and Campion (the latter wrote both words and music), was continued by composers such as William and Henry Lawes. The influence of writing for music can be seen in the uncharacteristically smooth versification of Donne's song 'Sweetest Love, I do not go', but is most apparent of all in the carefully structured, sweet sounding verse of Herbert. Walton wrote of him: 'His chiefest recreation was in music, in which heavenly art he was a most excellent master, and did himself compose many divine hymns and anthems, which he set and sung to his lute or viol.'

It was not a period in which English painting flourished greatly, but the great Elizabethan miniaturist Nicholas Hilliard was respected by Donne:

> a hand, or eye
> By Hilliard drawn, is worth an history,
> By a worse painter made.

('The Storm', 3–5)

Hilliard's well-known portrait of the 'Unknown Man' holding a locket of his beloved with a melancholy look in his eyes while the flames of love rage behind him represents well the Petrarchan attitude to love that Donne could both mock and sympathise with.

The Petrarchan approach to love was one which other poets also regarded with mixed feelings. Nearly two hundred years after they were written the sonnets of the Italian poet Petrarch (1304–74) to his beloved but unattainable Laura reached English through the translations and imitations of Wyatt and Surrey in the earlier part of the sixteenth century. The lyrical beauty of the sonnets was soon imitated, but their subtlety and strength of feeling were less easily captured. Soon the laments of the unhappy lover and his exaggerated admiration for his mistress provoked mockery from other poets (as in Hall's 'Satire 7', p. 166) and a different style of love poetry which laid stress on an unflattering sincerity, as in the opening of this sonnet by Shakespeare:

My mistress' eyes are nothing like the sun;
Coral is far more red than her lips' red;
If snow be white, why then her breasts are dun;
If hairs be wires, black wires grow on her head.

(Sonnet 130)

Donne's achievement was to take the conventions and give them fresh life. The effect is often humorous, but it is by no means mere parody:

As lightning or a taper's light,
Thine eyes, and not thy noise waked me.

('The Dream', 11–12)

If her eyes have not blinded thine.

('The Sun Rising', 15)

The literature of the whole of the period is remarkably rich, but it is possible to do no more than remind the reader of its two dominating figures. It could be argued that the dramatic qualities and psychological insight of Shakespeare find their match in miniature in Donne's poetry. If Shakespeare deals with love, ambition and evil in its more secular forms, then Milton tackles the religious concerns of the age in his attempt to 'justify the ways of God to men' in *Paradise Lost*. His concern with the consequences of man's sinful nature, with free will and predestination, and above all with man's hope of salvation, is shared by all the poets in this volume.

## The poets

A study of their careers will show how deeply involved in the affairs of their time Donne, Herbert and Marvell were. They were all of them men of wide education and interests and of considerable ambition and they were all, incidentally, Members of Parliament; not that that was particularly a path to power. It is also interesting to note that none of the three published volumes of poetry, as opposed to individual poems, during his life time. Herbert might well have done so if he had lived longer, but they did not think of themselves primarily as poets. This also explains the difficulty of some of the poetry, which was written for a circle of friends rather than for the public at large. Vaughan, the only one with no political ambitions, was in fact the only one to publish his own poetry.

**Donne** (1572–1631) was brought up in a Roman Catholic family that was very much involved in religious and political struggles, but in time he broke away from the faith of his youth and later still became an Anglican (see 'Satire 3' and its introduction). Such a break cannot have been easy and there must have been an element of defiance, even of daring, which it is hard for us to appreciate, in his disrespectful use of Catholic practices and beliefs as the imagery of such love poems as 'The Relic' and 'Twicknam Garden'. His change of church perhaps also helps to explain the uncertainty and fear of damnation in many of his religious poems.

He was educated at Oxford, but unable to take a degree as he was still a Catholic. He may have then gone to Cambridge and possibly travelled in Europe before going first to Thavies Inn and then, in 1592, to Lincoln's Inn. It was necessary to belong to one of the Inns of Court to become a lawyer, but the Inns also served as a kind of third English university, one situated furthermore in the capital. Donne read widely while he was there and was, according to a contemporary, Sir Richard Baker, 'a great visitor of ladies, a great frequenter of plays, a great writer of conceited verses'. He also met influential people such as the sons of his future employer, Sir Thomas Egerton.

It was after taking part in the naval expeditions to Cadiz and the Azores that he was employed by Sir Thomas, who as Lord Keeper of the Great Seal was a man of considerable influence. However a secret marriage to Ann More, his employer's wife's niece, led to his dismissal in 1602. There followed a long period of frustration, but finally he overcame hopes of secular advancement and a genuine sense of unworthiness, and was ordained in 1615. It is quite probable that Donne wrote most of the *Divine Meditations* during this interim period. In 1616 he was appointed Divinity Reader at Lincoln's Inn and the following year his wife died. In 1621 he was appointed Dean of St Paul's, a position he held until his death in 1631.

One of Donne's patrons was Magdalen Herbert, mother of **George Herbert** (1593–1633), and well known for her intellectual and literary interests. Herbert's own learning and his influential family connections led him to expect a successful public career like that of his brother, who was ambassador to Paris and later became Lord Herbert of Cherbury. Although his poetry smacks little of worldly matters his disappointment that this career failed to materialise is clear enough in a poem such as 'Affliction' (1). His early advance was rapid. As Public Orator of Cambridge University he was able to attract the attention of King James. He was also friendly with Francis Bacon, the Lord Chancellor, and he became MP for Montgomery. His career, however, went no further: Bacon was impeached; James died; and Herbert was still at Cambridge. In 1626 he was ordained deacon and finally in 1630 he was ordained priest and accepted the living at Bemerton near Salisbury. He led a life of outstanding piety there and in this final period wrote over half the poems in *The Temple* as well as revising the earlier ones. Taken together they can be seen as forming a spiritual autobiography revealing his struggles and disappointments and his final confidence in God's grace. In Donne's religious poetry the struggle still rages, but in Herbert's it has been resolved and there is a note of joyful praise in poems such as 'Easter' that is never heard in Donne.

In one sense the career of **Marvell** (1621–78) is the reverse of Herbert's, for he moved from a period of quiet retirement in his early thirties to public life. At that point he probably ceased to write poetry apart from a few occasional poems and political satires. The son of an Anglican clergyman he was educated at Cambridge and just after taking his BA degree in 1639 he had a brief conversion to Roman Catholicism. His father intervened, however, and sent him back to Cambridge. In the early 1640s he was evidently writing some lyrics since one of his poems was set to music by William Lawes, a Royalist who was killed at the siege of Chester in 1645. Marvell's own sympathies evidently changed since in 1653 he was recommended by Milton as Assistant Latin Secretary to the Council of State, although not appointed. It is to the four years prior to this that his best-known poems probably belong. They reveal the tension between the desire for a retired, private life and the sense that the demands of public life should not be resisted. The ironic detachment of Marvell's poetry makes it rash to treat the poems autobiographically, but in 1650 Marvell could write:

'Tis time to leave the books in dust,
And oil the unusèd armour's rust.

('An Horatian Ode', 5–6)

Nevertheless by the end of the year Marvell had joined Lord Fairfax, who had retired as commander of the New Model Army rather than invade Scotland, to act as tutor to his daughter. 'The Garden' makes clear how strongly Marvell felt the attractions of seclusion. In 1657, however, he became Milton's assistant as Latin Secretary to the Council of State and in 1659 he was elected MP for Hull, a position which he held for the rest of his life.

The quiet life that appealed to Marvell was a reality for **Henry Vaughan** (1621–95). Apart from four years spent probably at Oxford and then in London, almost his entire life was spent in Breconshire. All the same he was not altogether unaffected by the outside world. He was a royalist and may have briefly joined Colonel Price's company at Chester in 1645, and in 1650 his twin brother Thomas, a clergyman, was evicted from his living by the Puritans. Perhaps influenced by the royalist defeat and the death of his younger brother, William, Vaughan underwent a conversion, not in the sense of changing his church, but in letting his belief have a much more profound effect on his life. 'Regeneration' is one attempt to describe his experience. The change in the nature of his poetry in the two volumes of *Silex Scintillans* which he then published is striking not only in depth of feeling but also in quality. The major influence which he acknowledged in his preface and which is apparent throughout the two volumes is that of 'the blessed man, Mr George Herbert, whose holy life and verse gained many pious converts, (of whom I am the least)'. He chose the same sub-title that Herbert had used for *The Temple* – 'Sacred Poems and Private Ejaculations' – and like Herbert's book, *Silex Scintillans* is not simply devotional, but a form of spiritual autobiography.

One personal topic of poetry that Vaughan shared with all the poets of this period was death. Untimely death was common; but there was more to it than that. Death was not hidden in the nursing home and at the back of the crematorium, but accepted more openly. Donne's last sermon, 'Death's Duel', reminded his listeners that everyone must come to dust and 'be mingled with the dust of every highway, and of every dunghill, and swallowed in every puddle and pond'. Donne it was, too, who rose from his sick-bed to pose in his shroud for the drawing on which his funeral monument was to be based. (It can still be seen in the south aisle of St Paul's.)

## The poems

There is, I suppose, a danger that too much background material will merely seem to emphasise the differences between our own times and those of the metaphysical poets. It needs to be stressed, therefore, that the poems under consideration are alive and not fossils. Background knowledge may deepen our understanding and quicken our responses, but the poems can stand by themselves. The sceptical newcomer may object that the oldest of these poets was born over four hundred years ago and that his concerns cannot be ours, but Donne's uncomfortably honest treatment of death mentioned above is typical of his willingness to treat fundamental facts with the very honesty that we like to pride ourselves is particularly modern. In 'Satire 3' Donne's discussion of the different churches may seem remote to us, but we can sympathise with his contempt for those who unthinkingly accept others' ideas, and with his insistence that we should 'doubt wisely' but not passively:

To will, implies delay, therefore now do.
('Satire 3', 85)

The same rejection of received ideas is seen in his treatment of love. The Petrarchan convention of the sighing lover prostrate at the feet of his cruel mistress is never accepted at face value. If Donne is the unhappy lover he mocks himself for saying so in 'whining poetry' or comically exaggerates his feelings as in 'The Computation'. Where he does hark back to an earlier tradition it is to the sexually frank one of Ovid's elegies, viewing love with cynicism or imagining himself in bed with his mistress. His treatment of such themes remains, however, strikingly original as in 'The Dream' or 'The Sun Rising'. Marvell too can argue the case for love with vigour and humour in 'To His Coy Mistress' or write of it with subtly ambiguous detachment:

But sure as oft as women weep,
It is to be supposed they grieve.

('Mourning', 35–6)

The variety is considerable and includes occasionally in Donne's verse a tender simplicity which speaks directly to us:

Sweetest love, I do not go,
    For weariness of thee.

('Song', 1–2)

A number of the love poems also attempt an analysis of love's nature. Marvell's 'The Definition of Love' is more ingenious than convincing, but Vaughan in his 'Amoret' poems offers a description of the deeply seated attraction between lovers, and Donne offers a view of love which approaches the ideal when the platonic and sexual are combined:

But since my soul, whose child love is,
Takes limbs of flesh, and else could nothing do,
    More subtle than the parent is
Love must not be, but take a body too.

('Air and Angels', 7–10)

It is easy enough to see the continuing appeal of love poetry, but the religious poetry does offer more of a problem, especially to the non-Christian reader. It would be a mistake, however, to view these poems in a historical light as no more than evidence of a series of outmoded theological viewpoints. They are, above all, an account of *human* experience. Donne's fear that God does not love him enough to save him is not so very different from his fear that his mistress may leave him; indeed the imagery overlaps startlingly when he addresses God in these terms:

> for I
> Except you enthrall me, never shall be free,
> Nor ever chaste, except you ravish me.

(*Divine Meditations* 14, 12–14)

A number of Herbert's poems also give us a picture of struggle and doubts, even at times of bitter impatience:

> As good go any where, they say,
>     As to benumb
> Both knees and heart, in crying night and day,
>         *Come, come, my God, O come,*
>             But no hearing.

('Denial', 11–15)

Against these emotions can be set the rueful admission of self-interest in Marvell's 'The Coronet', the calm acceptance of death and hope of salvation at the end of Donne's 'Hymn to God my God in my Sickness' and the sheer elation of Herbert's 'Easter':

> Rise heart; thy Lord is risen. Sing his praise
>                 Without delays.

('Easter', 1–2)

There is also an interest in what makes man fully human. The interplay of mind and body that interests Donne in love poems like 'Air and Angels' and 'The Ecstasy' also concerns Marvell in 'A Dialogue between the Soul and Body'. Another topic which is common to both groups of poems is that of sincerity. Marvell recognises the danger of writing for the wrong motive in 'The Coronet', and just as Donne mocks the unconvincing language of love by exaggerating it, so Herbert sees the danger of being too ingenious:

> My thoughts began to burnish, sprout, and swell,
> Curling with metaphors a plain intention,
> Decking the sense, as if it were to sell.

('Jordan' (2), 4–6)

Other emotions we can understand and share are Vaughan's yearning for the innocence and vision of childhood ('The

Retreat'), Marvell's recognition of its vulnerability in the face of death ('The Picture of Little T. C.') and Vaughan's moving response to the sense of loss that death brings:

> They are all gone into the world of light!
>     And I alone sit lingering here.

('They are all gone', 1–2)

These emotions are common to us all, but the question that must now be answered is what makes these poems *uncommon*, metaphysical in fact. The word 'metaphysical' has become a useful label, but it is not in itself particularly helpful. Dryden once criticised Donne for 'affecting the metaphysics' in his love poetry, in other words 'perplexing the minds of the fair sex with nice [pedantic] speculations of philosophy'. Dr Johnson writing his *Life of Cowley* took up this accusation that Donne and a number of his successors were unduly philosophical, or metaphysical, and proceeded to coin the expression 'metaphysical poets' even while he pointed out that he did not consider them to be genuinely metaphysical!

There is in fact no single word or definition that can adequately sum up the range of poetry described as metaphysical. Donne was the great innovator, but those who followed had personalities, as well as minds, of their own and each poet's verse has its own distinctive quality. Personality, indeed, is a major factor, for much of the poetry expresses personal feelings as can be seen from the survey of its subject matter above. This is especially true of Donne and Herbert, although in the case of the latter the tone is calmer since the conflicts are seen in retrospect and the poet has their resolution in mind. (The conclusion of a poem like 'The Collar' may indeed seem too simple, but we come to realise that Herbert's calm is something that he has had to fight for.) The quieter, more meditative poems of Herbert and Vaughan also give the impression of a personal response to a specific situation or place:

> I made a posy, while the day ran by.

('Life', 1)

I cannot skill of these thy ways.

('Justice' (1), 1)

Dear stream! dear bank, where often I
Have sat, and pleased my pensive eye.

('The Waterfall', 13–14)

Marvell's great response to one particular place, 'Upon Appleton
House', is too long for inclusion in this anthology, but there is in
his poetry a sense of direct engagement in poems such as 'To His
Coy Mistress' and 'The Coronet'. There is also, however, a new
note of detachment in the thought-provoking ambiguity of 'An
Horatian Ode' or the unresolved conflict of 'A Dialogue between
the Soul and Body'.

We are aware, then, in most of this poetry of the individuality
of the poet, but it is not this in itself that makes the poetry
metaphysical. It is rather the way in which feeling is related to
thought that is the hallmark of the style. The personal feeling
gives an urgency to arguments which are often developed by
means of striking and extended analogies to a wide range of
things, sometimes learned, sometimes homely and often contemporary. With the possible exception of Vaughan, the imagery
is, in fact, used more for its logical than its emotional impact.
Very often the analogy or conceit seems improbable, but as the
poet works his idea out the reader is forced to accept its validity
and as he struggles to follow the reasoning (this is not poetry for
the passive reader) he gains new insight. It is frequently the
logical (or apparently logical) argument that gives shape and
structure to the whole poem.

Neither thought nor feeling could be adequately expressed,
however, if it were not for the remarkable adaptability and
variety of metaphysical versification. The harshness of 'Satire 3'
and the music of 'Virtue', the apparent disorder of 'The Collar'
and the suave smoothness of the couplets in 'To His Coy
Mistress' all have this in common: they are carefully calculated
to convey both logic and emotion.

Some poems are dominated by a single argument. 'To His Coy
Mistress', for example, is divided into three clear sections: if the

poet had time he would devote it to praising his mistress; but life is short; and so he reaches the conclusion: 'let us sport us while we may'. Each of the three sections is expanded and decorated with wit, but the structure stands out. Donne in 'The Flea' also presents a single argument to the same purpose, but the structure here is much denser, moving from the idea that the lovers are already united since their blood is mingled in the flea to the idea that the flea is their 'marriage bed' and 'temple'. Then when his mistress kills the flea to disprove his argument by implying that the blood the flea had sucked from her was of no importance, he switches the argument to suggest that she would lose no more honour than she had blood, if she complied with his wishes.

The image of the flea as the marriage temple is far fetched and comic, but other poems make more serious use of a single image in an extended conceit that again shapes the entire poem. Marvell's 'On a Drop of Dew' is devoted to the analogy between the drop of dew that has come from heaven and yearns to be drawn up to heaven again by the sun and the human soul which also yearns for heaven. Vaughan develops a similar idea in 'The Water-fall' which itself represents the death of the body, but not of the soul:

The common pass
Where, clear as glass,
All must descend
Not to an end.

(7–10)

The water then passes on to the sea where, like the soul, it is drawn up to heaven. Next Vaughan, unlike Marvell, changes the significance of his central image, moving to the water of baptism ('My sacred wash and cleanser') and on to the 'Fountains of life' and the memory of God's creative act when his Spirit moved upon the face of the waters and 'hatched all with his quickening love'.

The use of a single image, however, is the exception rather than the rule. In 'Vanity' (1) Herbert moves from the astronomer to the pearl diver to the chemist in successive verses, while Donne moves with bewildering rapidity in the first stanza of 'Twicknam

Garden' from transubstantiation to manna, to gall, to paradise and the serpent. Although the links are partly by association, they are also by logic. The same swift development is apparent in 'The Canonization':

Call us what you will, we are made such by love;
    Call her one, me another fly,
We are tapers too, and at our own cost die,
    And we in us find the eagle and the dove;
        The phoenix riddle hath more wit
        By us; we two being one, are it.
So to one neutral thing both sexes fit;
    We die and rise the same, and prove
    Mysterious by this love.

(19–27)

Each lover is like a fly attracted to a taper, but in that case each lover is a taper and burning away with love. By association the fly leads to the eagle and dove, symbols of strength and sweetness, and the combination of flames and birds leads naturally to the phoenix, which rises from the flames and which in its uniqueness is symbolic of their total union and unrivalled love. Finally the death and resurrection of the phoenix leads to the puns on 'die and rise' which suggest both the religious 'mystery' of their love and its sexuality ('die' is a slang term for achieving sexual satisfaction).

One aspect of metaphysical wit is the sheer range of imagery used. Donne may compare himself on his sick-bed to a map and Marvell describe ideal lovers as parallel lines; at the same time such ordinary things as the taper and the fly are brought in. Herbert in a fit of depression can claim that he is no more use than 'a blunted knife'. In some cases it is not the image that is original, but the use that is made of it. This is true in particular of a significant number of images in the religious poems which are already heavily laden with associations both from the Bible and from centuries of Christian usage.

One such image that has already been mentioned is that of water, and another that Vaughan makes much use of is light. Eternity is 'like a great *Ring* of pure and endless light' ('The

World' (1)) and 'God's saints are shining lights' who will show us the way to heaven and are indeed 'that City's shining spires' ('Joy of my life!'). Behind these images lie numerous Biblical references from the creation of light in *Genesis*, the very first act in creation, to Jesus's claim that he is 'the light of the world'. These references also support the recurring pun on sun and Son of God, as at the end of Herbert's 'Easter'. More startling, because less familiar, is the picture in 'The Agony' of Christ on the cross as a bunch of grapes being squeezed in the wine press of sin. The association is in fact a traditional one since Christ's blood is also the wine of the communion service or mass, and it is one of a number of instances where the modern reader may be mistaken in thinking that a poet is being typically 'daring' in the metaphysical manner. Herbert's achievement here is different; he has presented a meditation on Christ's agony in the Garden of Gethsemane which is moving in its description of a 'man so wrung with pains', but which is also carefully constructed to show in the second stanza the consequences of man's sin (i.e. Christ's suffering to redeem man) and in the third stanza that this suffering is Christ's love in action. The image of the wine press is used with insight to link Christ's broken bleeding body (the price of sin) with the joyful wine of redemption in the communion service:

Love is that liquor sweet and most divine,
Which my God feels as blood; but I, as wine.

(17–18)

Another aspect of Christian thinking which seems to fit naturally into the metaphysical style is paradox. Despite Christ's 'great birth' he is found among 'thieves and murderers' ('Redemption') and death is the gateway to life eternal. When Herbert asks Time to cut short his life because he is separated from God, Time replies:

This man deludes:
What do I here before his door?
He doth not crave less time, but more.

('Time', 28–30)

A paradox which is central to much of Herbert's poetry is that of a God who is both loving and cruel, and it is matched by the ambivalence of his own response which is sometimes loving and sometimes resentful. The twin ideas are expressed with apparent simplicity in the subtle structure of 'Bitter-Sweet'.

Ambivalence of this sort is also expressed by means of deliberate ambiguity. 'Affliction' (1) ends with these words:

Ah my dear God! though I am clean forgot,
Let me not love thee, if I love thee not.

(65–6)

At first sight Herbert appears to be pleading to be released from his ties to God, but the tone in which he addresses God and the uncertainty suggested by 'if' raise a doubt as to his intentions. Perhaps he is implying that he *does* love God after all. At this point the reader may realise that 'let' can mean hinder (it could still govern the infinitive in this sense in the seventeenth century), in which case the last line may mean: 'Even if I don't love you now, don't hinder me from loving you (in the future).' And so the puns and paradoxes imitated from the epigrams of Roman poets such as Martial cease to be trivial. Wit in the metaphysicals may be used for humour, but is usually directed to a serious purpose. At the end of each stanza of Donne's 'A Hymn to God the Father' ('When thou hast done; thou hast not done') the pun may strike the modern reader as comic, but there can be no doubt that Donne's self-examination, reviewing his sins, is serious.

Ambiguity of tone can also be used in a humorous way as well as a serious one. The opening of 'The Legacy' may sound sincere for a line or two despite its improbable opening statement, but the hyperbole and the extravagant image of the lovers' exchanged hearts soon make it clear that it is tongue-in-cheek. Marvell, too, is a master of calculated ambiguity. In 'The Garden' he talks of the paradisal delights of the garden, but strangely he uses the word 'Ensnared' and hints at the Fall:

Stumbling on melons, as I pass,
Ensnared with flowers, I fall on grass.

(39–40)

In 'An Horatian Ode' he is apparently praising Cromwell and yet doubts are placed in the reader's mind:

The forward youth that would appear
Must now forsake his muses dear.

(1–2)

Nevertheless Marvell has not forsaken his muses; he is writing poetry. Furthermore does 'forward' mean 'having proper ambition' or does it mean 'pushing and assertive'? The pun on 'plot' later in the poem throws a similar doubt; the man who looks after his garden plot is a man after Marvell's own heart, but what are his feelings about the man who engages in political plotting?

Wit of a simpler kind is to be found in another popular source of imagery, the emblem book. An emblem book contained a series of symbolic pictures, each with a motto and an explanatory verse with some kind of secular or religious moral. Vaughan used an emblem for the title page of *Silex Scintillans*. The title itself, which means 'sparkling flint', serves as a motto and above is a picture of a flint heart flaming where it has been struck by God's hand, but also weeping tears from a face that can be seen within it. A poem explains that Vaughan has been hard-hearted, but now God in his anger has struck the flint heart to produce flames of love from the sparks, and tears of remorse run down Vaughan's face. We are also told how Moses struck the rock in the desert to bring forth life-giving water. This type of symbolic image is to be found quite frequently in the poetry of Vaughan and Herbert. The anchor for hope in the poem of that name and the scales for judgement in 'Regeneration' are typical examples. Both these poems are allegories, although 'Hope' is a very compressed one. They depend, in fact, on a whole series of emblematic symbols for the development of their meaning. In addition Vaughan's 'The Water-fall' could be seen as the explanatory poem for an emblem picturing a waterfall.

A visual image appears very obviously in Herbert's 'Easter Wings', but there is more to it than just the immediate appearance of the poem. In each verse the decline of the poet's condition leads to the shortest lines ('Most poor', 'Most thin') and then the words 'With thee' introduce a swelling of the verse form as Herbert is raised on angel wings from misfortune to new hope:

Affliction shall advance the flight in me.

(20)

This delight in pattern and the use of it to underline the meaning is frequently to be found in Herbert's poetry. It can be seen in the careful interlinking of each line with its predecessor to suggest the structure of 'The Wreath' (and also in Vaughan's poem of the same title) and it can be seen in a poem like 'Virtue' where the recurrence of the simple pattern stresses the inevitability of death:

My music shows ye have your closes,
              And all must die.

(11–12)

In 'Denial' it is the completion of the rhyme scheme in the final stanza after its incompleteness in the earlier stanzas that offers new hope:

That so thy favours granting my request,
              They and my mind may chime,
              And mend my rhyme.

(28–30)

The 'music' of Herbert's verse never becomes automatic. He is always prepared to break the rhythm where appropriate to drive home the meaning as here in 'Denial' where he expresses both despair:

Then was my heart broken, as was my verse

(3)

and anger:

              O that thou shouldst give dust a tongue
                        To cry to thee,
        And then not hear it crying! all day long
                   My heart was in my knee,
                        But no hearing.

(16–20)

This staccato outburst with its terse and disgruntled conclusion has something of the dramatic quality which is found above all in Donne with his aggressive assertions and challenging rhetorical questions. Here too the effect depends very much on the breaking of the normal rhythmic patterns coupled with the use of idiomatic language. In 'The Sun Rising' there is a heavy stress on the opening syllable of the shock opening:

Busy old fool, unruly sun.

In *Divine Meditations* 7 the relentless forward motion of a breathless account of Judgement Day is maintained by running the sense on from the end of each line:

At the round earth's imagined corners, blow
Your trumpets, angels, and arise, arise
From death, you numberless infinities
Of souls, and to your scattered bodies go.

(1–4)

In *Divine Meditations* 14 there is not only the shock opening, but a string of heavily accented monosyllabic verbs in succession to suggest the vigorous action needed. This is not simply an unrestrained outburst of verbal energy for it is carefully structured. Each verb in line 2 is replaced by a more forceful one in line 4 since God, the blacksmith of Donne's heart, must not 'seek to mend', but must 'make [him] new':

Batter my heart, three-personed God; for, you
As yet but knock, breathe, shine, and seek to mend;
That I may rise, and stand, o'erthrow me, and bend
Your force, to break, blow, burn, and make me new.

(1–4)

The stressing of the paradox in line 3 by the deliberate juxtaposition of 'stand' and 'o'erthrow' is further evidence of the care with which Donne organises his verse.

The poetry of Marvell is not as ruggedly dramatic as that of Donne. Nevertheless the tone of the spoken voice can still be heard in his poetry. At times it is suavely ironic and best expressed in the smoothness of a polished couplet:

The grave's a fine and private place,
But none, I think, do there embrace.

('To His Coy Mistress', 31–2)

At other times a sudden sense of urgency breaks into the rhythm:

But at my back I always hear
Time's wingèd chariot hurrying near.

(21–2)

In 'A Dialogue between the Soul and Body' the somewhat abstract subject is brought to life in an acrimonious debate in which the Soul sneers at the Body, stressing its inadequacies with a series of paradoxes ('fettered stands/In feet; and manacled in hands') and complaining of both the Body's sickness and its health:

Constrained not only to endure
Diseases, but, what's worse, the cure.

(27–8)

The Body gives as good as it gets and interestingly is left with the last word. Not only is the tone wittily contemptuous with its rhetorical question, but also the Body is given one of Marvell's strongest images; the natural innocence of the Body before it is corrupted by the Soul's sin is compared to the greenness of Nature before it is harmed by man:

What but a soul could have the wit
To build me up for sin so fit?
So architects do square and hew
Green trees that in the forest grew.

(41–4)

Here indeed is a poem which is literally metaphysical in its subject matter. In the satirical tone of its rhyming couplets it might be thought to look forward to the Augustan satire that was to follow and yet it is also metaphysical in the poetic sense. Some of Donne's earliest poetry in the 1590s had been satirical and that too had been typically metaphysical in its dramatic style, blending wit and feeling, and using complexity of expression to mirror complexity of thought.

It is finally to Donne, the originator, that we must return. In the words of Thomas Carew's elegy he 'opened us a mine/Of rich and pregnant fancy' and drew 'a line/Of masculine expression':

The Muses' garden with pedantic weeds
O'erspread, was purged by thee; the lazy seeds
Of servile imitation thrown away,
And fresh invention planted, thou didst pay
The debts of our penurious bankrupt age . . .
Here lies a King, that ruled as he thought fit
The universal monarchy of wit.

(25–9, 95–6)

### Further reading
*Editions*

The following editions are not only cheap and easily available, but good. The three Penguins have very thorough notes and the Herbert fewer notes but an interesting introduction.

E. S. Donno (ed.), *Andrew Marvell, The Complete Poems*. Penguin, 1972

C. A. Patrides (ed.), *The English Poems of George Herbert*. Dent, 1974

Alan Rudrum (ed.), *Henry Vaughan, The Complete Poems*. Penguin, 1976

A. J. Smith (ed.), *John Donne, The Complete English Poems*. Penguin, 1971

Another very interesting edition is:

Theodore Redpath, *The Songs and Sonnets of John Donne*. Methuen, 1983

### Anthologies

John Broadbent (ed.), *Poets of the 17th Century* (2 vols.). Signet, 1974 (wide-ranging and includes non-metaphysical poetry)

Helen Gardner (ed.), *The Metaphysical Poets*, Penguin, 1957 (brief but excellent introduction)

## Literary histories

Boris Ford (ed.), *From Donne to Marvell*, vol. 3 of *The New Pelican Guide to English Literature*. Penguin, 1982

Bruce King, *Seventeenth-Century English Literature*. Macmillan, 1982

Christopher Ricks (ed.), *English Poetry and Prose, 1540–1674*, vol. 2 of *Sphere History of Literature in the English Language*. Sphere, 1970

Also useful for background information is:

Isabel Rivers, *Classical and Christian Ideas in English Renaissance Poetry*. George Allen and Unwin, 1979

## Critical studies

The following very brief list is only meant to provide a few starting points in the immense amount of material available. (There is, of course, no substitute for detailed study of the poems themselves.)

A good introductory study with chapters on all four poets is:

Joan Bennett, *Five Metaphysical Poets*. Cambridge University Press, 1964

W. R. Keast (ed.), *Seventeenth-Century English Poetry*. Oxford University Press, 1962 (contains essays by H. J. C. Grierson, T. S. Eliot, Helen Gardner and many others)

### Donne

John Carey, *John Donne: Life, Mind and Art*. Faber, 1981 (very good on the link between life and poetry)

James Winny, *A Preface to Donne*. Longman, revised edition 1981

### Herbert
Margaret Bottrall, *George Herbert*. Murray, 1954 (combines biography with critical study)

Rosemond Tuve, *A Reading of George Herbert*. Chicago, 1952

### Marvell

John Carey (ed.), *Andrew Marvell, A Critical Anthology*. Penguin, 1969

*Vaughan*

E. C. Pettett, *Of Paradise and Light*. Cambridge University Press, 1960

## Other reading

Dr Johnson's comments on metaphysical poetry in his 'Life of Cowley' (*Lives of the English Poets*) are still stimulating as is the approach of William Empson in *Seven Types of Ambiguity* (Chatto & Windus, 1930, reissued Penguin, 1973). It is also valuable to follow up biblical references in the notes to establish the context of the references. Try also to attend a church where the *Book of Common Prayer* is still used to get the feel of liturgical language in action.

# John Donne
## 1572–1631

## Air and Angels

Twice or thrice had I lovèd thee,
Before I knew thy face or name;
So in a voice, so in a shapeless flame,
Angels affect us oft, and worshipped be;
   Still when, to where thou wert, I came,       5
Some lovely glorious nothing I did see,
   But since my soul, whose child love is,
Takes limbs of flesh, and else could nothing do,
   More subtle than the parent is
Love must not be, but take a body too,       10
   And therefore what thou wert, and who
      I bid love ask, and now
That it assume thy body, I allow,
And fix itself in thy lip, eye, and brow.

Whilst thus to ballast love, I thought,       15
And so more steadily to have gone,
With wares which would sink admiratiön,
I saw, I had love's pinnace overfraught,
   Every thy hair for love to work upon
Is much too much, some fitter must be sought;      20
   For, nor in nothing, nor in things
Extreme, and scatt'ring bright, can love inhere;
   Then as an angel, face and wings
Of air, not pure as it, yet pure doth wear,
   So thy love may be my love's sphere;      25
      Just such disparity
As is 'twixt air and angels' purity,
'Twixt women's love, and men's will ever be.

This is one of Donne's most difficult poems and the newcomer to his poetry is advised to start elsewhere and return to this poem later. In it Donne argues that neither a purely platonic love (see introduction) nor one based solely on his mistress's physical beauty can satisfactorily be sustained. His love can only be completely fulfilled if his mistress will respond.

3 **So** just as; he has fallen in love with the platonic ideal before he has seen her in the flesh, just as men can be influenced by, and pay respect to, angels without their taking any specific form.

5–6 Whenever he came into her presence he remained conscious not of her body, but of the platonic ideal which is radiantly bright ('lovely glorious') although it has no physical presence ('nothing').

7–10 Just as the soul has to work through the body, so love, which is the 'child' of the soul, must also 'take a body'.

8 **else** otherwise.

9 **subtle** lacking in physical substance; perhaps also cunning.

13 **That . . . allow** I permit my love ('it') to lay claim to, or to put on ('assume') your body. (His soul must function through his own body; his love through his mistress's body.) A subsidiary meaning of 'assume' is perhaps 'take up into heaven'; if so the soul has not 'descended' to the body, but raised it up to its own spiritual level.

15–18 Her physical charms are to steady his love just as a cargo of goods ('wares') provides the ballast to make a light boat ('pinnace') sail more steadily, but so many are her charms that the boat of his love is overloaded ('overfraught') and in danger of sinking.

17 **admiratiön** five syllables.

19 **Every thy hair** every one of your hairs.

20 **some fitter** some fitter dwelling place for love.

21–2 **For . . . inhere** Love cannot dwell in/be sustained by ('inhere' in) either the platonic ideal that lacks physical substance ('nothing'), or her radiant outward beauties.

23–5 To make themselves visible to men angels assume a body of condensed air (the purest of the four elements but not as pure as angels themselves); similarly his love will 'inhere' in/find its form in her love. A second comparison is implied by 'sphere'; each heavenly body was thought to be a sphere inhabited and controlled by an angel or intelligence. Compare 'The Ecstasy', lines 51–2 and 57–8 (p35).

6–8 There is a difference in the quality of their loves just as air, although pure, is not as pure as an angel. The implication would seem to be that the man's initiating love is slightly superior to that of the woman, but nevertheless dependent on it in order to become fully realised.

# The Canonization

For God's sake hold your tongue, and let me love,
    Or chide my palsy, or my gout,
My five grey hairs, or ruined fortune flout,
    With wealth your state, your mind with arts improve,
        Take you a course, get you a place,         5
        Observe his Honour, or his Grace,
Or the King's real, or his stampèd face
    Contemplate; what you will, approve,
    So you will let me love.

Alas, alas, who's injured by my love?         10
    What merchant's ships have my sighs drowned?
Who says my tears have overflowed his ground?
    When did my colds a forward spring remove?
        When did the heats which my veins fill
        Add one more to the plaguy bill?         15
Soldiers find wars, and lawyers find out still
    Litigious men, which quarrels move,
    Though she and I do love.

Call us what you will, we are made such by love;
    Call her one, me another fly,         20
We are tapers too, and at our own cost die,
    And we in us find the eagle and the dove;
        The Phoenix riddle hath more wit
        By us; we two being one, are it.
So to one neutral thing both sexes fit;         25
    We die and rise the same, and prove
    Mysterious by this love.

We can die by it, if not live by love,
    And if unfit for tombs and hearse
Our legend be, it will be fit for verse;          30
    And if no piece of chronicle we prove,
      We'll build in sonnets pretty rooms;
      As well a well wrought urn becomes
The greatest ashes, as half-acre tombs,
    And by these hymns, all shall approve     35
    Us canonized for love:

And thus invoke us; 'You whom reverend love
    Made one another's hermitage;
You, to whom love was peace, that now is rage;
    Who did the whole world's soul contract, and drove    40
      Into the glasses of your eyes
      (So made such mirrors, and such spies,
That they did all to you epitomize)
    Countries, towns, courts: beg from above
    A pattern of your love!'         45

**Canonization** formal recognition as a saint, but here in the religion of love.

2 **Or . . . gout** Rebuke me for suffering either from palsy (a form of paralysis that causes trembling) or from gout (inflammation of the joints). Both diseases improbably suggest that Donne is approaching old age; compare 'My five grey hairs' in line 3.

3 **flout** mock.

4 **state** estate.
**arts** learning.

5 **Take you a course** follow a career or perhaps take a course of medical treatment.
**a place** a place at court.

6 Pay obsequious attention to someone of noble rank in the hope of winning favour.

7 **real** real *and* royal.
**stamped** i.e. on a coin.

7–8 **Or . . . Contemplate** Be a courtier or a money-maker.

8 **approve** try.

9 **So** so long as.

10–15 A series of extravagant love images which might suggest that his love was harmful are dismissed: 'sighs' are not tempests, nor 'tears' floods; coldness in love does not check an early ('forward') spring, nor does hot passion lengthen the list of plague dead ('the plaguy bill').

17 **Litigious ... move** men eager to take legal action who stir up quarrels.

20–1 Just as the moth is attracted to its destruction in the candle so they are attracted to destruction in the fires of passion. They are candles ('tapers') which consume themselves as they burn ('at our own cost die'). To 'die' is also a common expression of the time for achieving sexual satisfaction; this meaning is relevant both here and later.

22 **the eagle and the dove** masculine vigour and feminine gentleness.

23–7 In their perfect union the lovers become one flesh, which is of neither sex ('neutral'), as is the only phoenix that exists at any time, the new phoenix rising from the ashes of the previous one. The 'phoenix riddle' is symbolic of resurrection and the lovers' union is 'mysterious' (a religious mystery) when they 'die and rise'; the sexual and religious implications of these last words provide the turning point from earthly love to canonization.

30 **legend** story of a saint's life.

31 **chronicle** history.

33–4 **As ... tombs** The well made urn is as fitting a container of a great man's remains as a huge tomb.

35 **hymns** i.e. the sonnets which are hymns in the religion of love.

37 **invoke us** Later lovers are to pray to them just as Roman Catholics would pray to saints to intercede to God on their behalf.

38 **hermitage** The hermit (holy man) lives alone just as the lovers lived only in each other.

39 Later lovers, whose love is 'rage', look back to the 'peace' of the 'canonized' couple's ideal love.

40–4 The lovers were the whole world to each other. Their eyes were 'spies' that saw everything reflected in the eyes ('mirrors') of the beloved.

44–5 **beg ... love** Pray to the God of Love to give us a copy ('pattern') of your love. A 'pattern' is an example to be imitated.

# The Computation

For the first twenty years, since yesterday,
   I scarce believed, thou couldst be gone away,
For forty more, I fed on favours past,
   And forty on hopes, that thou wouldst, they might last.
Tears drowned one hundred, and sighs blew out two,     5
   A thousand, I did neither think, nor do,
   Or not divide, all being one thought of you;
   Or in a thousand more, forgot that too.
Yet call not this long life; but think that I
Am, by being dead, immortal; can ghosts die?     10

   **The Computation** turns 24 hours into 2,400 years!
4 **that thou wouldst** that you wanted (to continue your favours).
8 **forgot that too** He is so overcome that he cannot even remember her.
10 **dead** killed by his unhappy love.

# The Dream

Dear love, for nothing less than thee
Would I have broke this happy dream,
       It was a theme
For reason, much too strong for fantasy,
Therefore thou waked'st me wisely; yet     5
My dream thou brok'st not, but continued'st it;
Thou art so true, that thoughts of thee suffice,
To make dreams truths, and fables histories;
Enter these arms, for since thou thought'st it best,
Not to dream all my dream, let's act the rest.     10

As lightning, or a taper's light,
Thine eyes, and not thy noise waked me;
       Yet I thought thee
(For thou lov'st truth) an angel, at first sight,
But when I saw thou saw'st my heart,     15

And knew'st my thoughts, beyond an angel's art,
When thou knew'st what I dreamed, when thou knew'st when
Excess of joy would wake me, and cam'st then,
I must confess, it could not choose but be
Profane, to think thee anything but thee.                    20

Coming and staying showed thee, thee,
But rising makes me doubt, that now,
                    Thou art not thou.
That love is weak, where fear's as strong as he;
'Tis not all spirit, pure, and brave,                        25
If mixture it of fear, shame, honour, have.
Perchance as torches which must ready be,
Men light and put out, so thou deal'st with me,
Thou cam'st to kindle, goest to come; then I
Will dream that hope again, but else would die.              30

3    **theme** subject.

4    'Reason' functions when he is awake; 'fantasy' when he dreams.

7    **true** not only loyal, but an embodiment of truth itself; an early
     pointer, perhaps, to the near blasphemous hint of a comparison to
     God in the next stanza.

11–12  Compare 'The Sun Rising', line 15 (p47).

15–20  When he saw that she understood his thoughts and feelings with a
       skill ('art') greater than an angel's it could only have been
       blasphemous ('profane') to think her anything but herself (since
       otherwise to possess such knowledge she would have had to be God).

21   **showed thee, thee** proved you to be yourself.

22   **rising** i.e. to leave the bed.

24–6  It is a poor love that does not drive out all other considerations.

27–8  Torches which must be 'ready' for immediate use are lit in advance
      and then extinguished so that they can be lit easily when the need
      arises.

29   **kindle** not only the lighting of the torch, but also sexual arousal.
     **goest to come** leave with the intention of returning.

30   **die** The meaning is sexual as in 'The Canonization'.

# The Ecstasy

Where, like a pillow on a bed,
   A pregnant bank swelled up, to rest
The violet's reclining head,
   Sat we two, one another's best;

Our hands were firmly cemented        5
   With a fast balm, which thence did spring,
Our eye-beams twisted, and did thread
   Our eyes, upon one double string;

So to intergraft our hands, as yet
   Was all our means to make us one,      10
And pictures in our eyes to get
   Was all our propagatiön.

As 'twixt two equal armies, Fate
   Suspends uncertain victory,
Our souls (which to advance their state,    15
   Were gone out) hung 'twixt her, and me.

And whilst our souls negotiate there,
   We like sepulchral statues lay;
All day, the same our postures were,
   And we said nothing, all the day.     20

If any, so by love refined,
   That he soul's language understood,
And by good love were grown all mind,
   Within convenient distance stood,

He (though he knew not which soul spake   25
   Because both meant, both spake the same)
Might thence a new concoction take,
   And part far purer than he came.

This ecstasy doth unperplex
   (We said) and tell us what we love,    30
We see by this, it was not sex,
   We see, we saw not what did move:

But as all several souls contain
   Mixture of things, they know not what,
Love, these mixed souls doth mix again,        35
   And makes both one, each this and that.

A single violet transplant,
   The strength, the colour, and the size
(All which before was poor, and scant)
   Redoubles still, and multiplies.        40

When love, with one another so
   Interinanimates two souls,
That abler soul, which thence doth flow,
   Defects of loneliness controls.

We then, who are this new soul, know,        45
   Of what we are composed, and made,
For, the atomies of which we grow,
   Are souls, whom no change can invade.

But O alas, so long, so far
   Our bodies why do we forbear?        50
They are ours, though they are not we, we are
   The intelligences, they the sphere.

We owe them thanks, because they thus
   Did us, to us, at first convey,
Yielded their forces, sense, to us,        55
   Nor are dross to us, but allay.

On man heaven's influence works not so,
   But that it first imprints the air,
So soul into the soul may flow,
   Though it to body first repair.        60

As our blood labours to beget
   Spirits, as like souls as it can,
Because such fingers need to knit
   That subtle knot, which makes us man:

So must pure lovers' souls descend        65
   To affections, and to faculties,

Which sense may reach and apprehend,
    Else a great prince in prison lies.

To our bodies turn we then, that so
    Weak men on love revealed may look;                    70
Love's mysteries in souls do grow,
    But yet the body is his book.

And if some lover, such as we,
    Have heard this dialogue of one,
Let him still mark us, he shall see                        75
    Small change, when we're to bodies gone.

---

**Ecstasy** A technical term for the taking up of the soul from the body in a religious trance; *not* the modern meaning.

1–4 Just as the poem as a whole argues that platonic love should be combined with physical love, so the setting for the lovers' meeting combines a pastoral innocence (the 'violet' suggests faithfulness and humility) with the sensual suggestiveness of 'pregnant' and 'pillow'.

5 **cemented** stress on first syllable.

6 **balm** their sweat, but also a preservative medicine which keeps them firmly united ('fast').

8 **one double string** The paradox that the string is both one and double stresses that the two lovers are one.

9 **intergraft** graft on each other (like two plants).

10 Holding hands was the only 'means' that they had used to achieve physical union.

11–12 Instead of having children they had only created reflections of themselves in each other's eyes ('get' = beget).

14 **Suspends** Victory hangs in the balance.

15–16 In their mutual ecstasy the souls have left the bodies, just as ambassadors go ahead of an army to advance its cause.

18 **like sepulchral statues** like the statues of husband and wife on a funeral monument.

23 a reference to the spiritualising effect of love according to platonic theory (see introduction).

27 **a new concoction take** experience a new refinement to something more precious (cf. line 21), like metal in a furnace; according to alchemists gold had perfect concoction. Compare Herbert's 'The Elixir' (p85).

29  **unperplex**  make clear; enlightenment comes to the soul while it is in
    ecstasy.

32  **We . . . move**  We see that we previously failed to understand the
    power that moved us to love.

33–6  **But . . . that**  Each individual ('several') soul is a mixture, and love has
    mixed the two mixtures ('these mixed souls doth mix again') to make
    'both one', each soul possessing the qualities of both souls. This is
    perhaps a 'concoction' (line 27).

37–40  Transplanting a violet improves its qualities; the same applies to a
    soul.

40  **still**  continually.

42  **Interinanimates**  The two souls give life to each other and are
    blended together. ('Anima' is the Latin for 'soul'.)

43–4  The more powerful soul, which derives from the interinanimation of
    the two souls, can put right the weaknesses of either soul in isolation.

45–8  Souls, unlike bodies, do not die or change and, since the components
    ('atomies') of the lovers' 'new soul' are their undying souls, it, and by
    implication their love, cannot die.

50  **forbear**  refrain from using.

51–2  **They . . . sphere**  We are more than just our bodies (since we have
    souls). The body is controlled by the soul as a heavenly sphere is by
    its intelligence or angel.

53  **them**  their bodies.

55  **forces, sense**  physical strength and the five senses.

56  The image is again of refining metal. The body is not a pure
    'concoction', but nor is it the valueless scum ('dross') on the top of
    the molten ore. It is an alloy ('allay') that has its part to play.

57–8  An angel must take a body of air to be visible to man; or, the
    'influence' (a technical term in astrology) of the stars is transmitted
    by the air.

60  **repair**  go.

61  **beget**  produce.

62  **Spirits**  The natural, animal and vital spirits were fluids produced by
    the blood which made possible the link between soul and body.
    There is perhaps a pun here since the blood – often associated with
    sexual passion as in 'The Flea' (p38) – is labouring to produce
    something spiritual, while the souls are to 'descend' to bodily things.

64 **That subtle knot**  the mysterious linking of body and soul that makes possible a living man.

66 **Affections**  emotions.
   **faculties**  physical functions.

67 **Which . . . apprehend**  which the bodily senses may reach up to and grasp; the whole being, body and soul, is thus involved in love.

68 **Else**  otherwise.
   **a great prince**  their love; if their love does not use the agency of their bodies, just as a prince must govern through the agency of his inferiors, then it is impotent ('in prison') or it is incapable of being set free and achieving the fulfilment that occurs when 'soul into the soul may flow'. Alternatively the 'prince' is perhaps the unborn child imprisoned in the womb.

69–70 Just as God is revealed in the person of Jesus ('the Word made flesh') so in the religion of Love doubters ('Weak men') will have true love revealed to them.

71 **mysteries**  the sacred secrets of the religion of Love.

72 **book**  the outward sign and explanation of Love's mysteries.

74 Compare lines 25–6.

75 **mark**  watch.

76 **when we're to bodies gone**  not only when their love becomes physical, but when their ecstasy is ended; thus the poem is brought to its conclusion.

# The Flea

Mark but this flea, and mark in this,
How little that which thou deny'st me is;
Me it sucked first, and now sucks thee,
And in this flea, our two bloods mingled be;
Confess it, this cannot be said                    5
A sin, or shame, or loss of maidenhead,
    Yet this enjoys before it woo,
    And pampered swells with one blood made of two,
    And this, alas, is more than we would do.

Oh stay, three lives in one flea spare,                                    10
Where we almost, nay more than married are.
This flea is you and I, and this
Our marriage bed, and marriage temple is;
Though parents grudge, and you, we're met,
And cloistered in these living walls of jet.                               15
   Though use make you apt to kill me,
   Let not to this, self murder added be,
   And sacrilege, three sins in killing three.

Cruel and sudden, hast thou since
Purpled thy nail, in blood of innocence?                                   20
In what could this flea guilty be,
Except in that drop which it sucked from thee?
Yet thou triumph'st, and say'st that thou
Find'st not thyself, nor me the weaker now;
   'Tis true, then learn how false, fears be;                  25
   Just so much honour, when thou yield'st to me,
   Will waste, as this flea's death took life from thee.

1 **Mark but** just look at.
  **mark in this** learn from this.

4 It was thought that the blood of lovers was mingled in the sexual act.
  The poet implies that there is no point in the woman refusing his
  advances since their blood is already mingled.

10 **Oh stay** stop (i.e. don't kill it).

15 **cloistered** shut up; a comic word to use in this context, given its
   suggestion of chaste seclusion in a monastery.
   **living walls of jet** the cloister walls are in fact the black skin of the
   flea.

16 **use** habit (of killing me by unkindness).

18 **sacrilege** Just as it would be a crime against religion ('sacrilege') to
   attack the Trinity of Father, Son and Holy Ghost, so it is a crime to kill
   the three-in-one of the flea, poet and woman.

19 **since** already.

.5–7 The woman's mocking rejection of the poet's argument in the
   previous stanza is turned against her. She will lose no more honour
   in yielding to him than she lost life when the flea was killed.

# The Good Morrow

I wonder by my troth, what thou, and I
   Did, till we loved? were we not weaned till then,
But sucked on country pleasures, childishly?
   Or snorted we in the seven sleepers' den?
'Twas so; but this, all pleasures fancies be.         5
If ever any beauty I did see,
Which I desired, and got, 'twas but a dream of thee.

And now good morrow to our waking souls,
   Which watch not one another out of fear;
For love, all love of other sights controls,       10
   And makes one little room, an everywhere.
Let sea-discoverers to new worlds have gone,
Let maps to others, worlds on worlds have shown,
Let us possess one world, each hath one, and is one.

My face in thine eye, thine in mine appears,      15
   And true plain hearts do in the faces rest,
Where can we find two better hemispheres
   Without sharp north, without declining west?
Whatever dies, was not mixed equally;
If our two loves be one, or, thou and I        20
Love so alike, that none do slacken, none can die.

1  **by my troth**  by my faith; a way of giving added emphasis to the forceful, colloquial tone of the opening.

2–3  **were . . . childishly**  Were we like babies who were fed on nothing but the milk of innocent ('country') pleasures? To the town-dweller the country seems unsophisticated, but perhaps there is sexual innuendo as in Hamlet's question to Ophelia: 'Do you think I meant country matters?' (*Hamlet*, Act 3 Scene 2).

4  **seven sleepers**  seven young Christians who were walled up in a cave during the persecutions and who reportedly slept for nearly two hundred years.

5  **but this, all pleasures fancies be**  All pleasures apart from this (their love) are mere illusions.

6–7  The beauty of previous mistresses was only ('but') a foreshadowing of her beauty.

8 **good morrow**  He greets their souls who have just woken up to what true love is.

9–10  They watch one another out of love, not suspicion, since love stops them wishing to see anything but each other.

11  They are all the world to each other and so the 'little room' where they are is 'an everywhere'.

12–13 **Let . . . shown**  Never mind if explorers have found new lands and star maps have shown new stars. The form of the verbs ('Let sea-discoverers . . . have gone' and 'Let maps . . . have shown') is unfamiliar, but is simply the past tense of 'let them go' and 'let them show'.

14  The lovers dismiss the 'worlds' of contemporary discovery because each possesses a world in the beloved and is a world to the beloved. Because of their unity in love these worlds are 'one world'.

16  Their loving looks are not deceitful.

17 **hemispheres**  the halves of the eyes that can be seen reflecting each other as well as the two perfectly matching halves of their 'one world'.

18  Their microcosm (miniature model epitomizing the outside world or macrocosm) is in fact superior to the real world, for it lacks the cold ('sharp') North of ill feeling and the setting ('declining') sun of love that decays.

19–21  There was a medical theory that disease and death could only occur when the humours (constituent elements of the body) were not in exact balance against each other. Since their two loves are 'one' they must be identical and equally balanced and so their mutual love cannot die.


# The Legacy

When I died last (and, dear, I die
   As often as from thee I go),
   Though it be an hour ago,
And lovers' hours be full eternity,
I can remember yet, that I
   Something did say, and something did bestow;

5

Though I be dead, which sent me, I should be
Mine own executor and legacy.

I heard me say: 'Tell her anon,
    That my self' (that is you, not I)                    10
        'Did kill me'; and when I felt me die,
I bid me send my heart, when I was gone;
But I alas could there find none,
    When I had ripped me, and searched where hearts should
        lie;
It killed me again, that I who still was true             15
In life, in my last will should cozen you.

Yet I found something like a heart,
    But colours it, and corners had,
    It was not good, it was not bad,
It was entire to none, and few had part.                 20
As good as could be made by art
    It seemed; and therefore for our losses sad,
I meant to send this heart instead of mine,
But oh, no man could hold it, for 'twas thine.

 6  What he said is revealed in lines 9–11 and what he bestowed was the
    legacy of his heart (line 12).

7–8 **which . . . legacy** which (the act of remembering) told me that I
    should be the executor of my own will and the gift bequeathed in it;
    'me' is an indirect object: 'sent word *to me* that . . .'

 9  **anon** at once, or soon.

10  In an ideal love the lovers are so united that each is the other and so
    the poet can call his mistress 'my self'. This love, however, is clearly
    not ideal.

12  I told myself to send my heart when I was dead.

15  **who still was true** who always kept my word.

16  **cozen** trick.

17  Just as the lovers are each other (line 10), so they have exchanged
    hearts, but what she has given him is only 'something like a heart'.

18  **colours** deceitful outward appearance: it is only a symbolic heart
    painted in heraldic 'colours'. There is perhaps also a reference to his

mistress's deceptive use of figures of speech ('colours') like those in the poem itself.

**corners**  sharp hurtful edges, or a lack of straightforwardness?

20  **It . . . part**  Nobody had all of it and few had any share of it at all.

24  **no man could hold it, for 'twas thine**  The heart was too slippery to be sent *because* it was hers. No man can hold her affection because she is unfaithful by nature.

# The Relic

When my grave is broke up again
Some second guest to entertain,
(For graves have learned that woman-head
To be to more than one a bed)
And he that digs it, spies                                5
A bracelet of bright hair about the bone,
Will he not let us alone,
And think that there a loving couple lies,
Who thought that this device might be some way
To make their souls, at the last busy day,               10
Meet at this grave, and make a little stay?

If this fall in a time, or land,
Where mis-devotion doth command,
Then, he that digs us up, will bring
Us, to the Bishop, and the King,                         15
To make us relics; then
Thou shalt be a Mary Magdalene, and I
A something else thereby;
All women shall adore us, and some men;
And since at such time, miracles are sought,             20
I would have that age by this paper taught
What miracles we harmless lovers wrought.

First, we loved well and faithfully,
Yet knew not what we loved, nor why,
Difference of sex no more we knew,                       25

Than our guardian angels do;
          Coming and going, we
Perchance might kiss, but not between those meals;
          Our hands ne'er touched the seals,
Which nature, injured by late law, sets free:                    30
These miracles we did; but now alas,
All measure, and all language, I should pass,
Should I tell what a miracle she was.

**Relic**  part of saint's body or possessions held in veneration.

2  **second guest**  another body in a crowded graveyard.

3–4  Notice the witty distinction implied between 'woman-head' (womanly behaviour) and maidenhead.

6  The 'bracelet' is a love token.

9–11  The 'device' is the linking of their earthly remains so that at the resurrection of the body on 'the last busy day' (the Day of Judgement) they may meet and pause briefly ('make a little stay').

12  **fall**  should happen.

13  **Where . . . command**  where the mistaken Roman Catholic practice of venerating relics is prevalent (but here it is the religion of love).

17  **Mary Magdalene**  a reformed prostitute who became a follower of Christ.

18  **a something else**  possibly one of Mary Magdalene's earlier lovers, but much more probably the poem verges on blasphemy hinting that the poet is a Christ figure before backing away from the idea. Compare the second stanza of 'The Dream' (p32).

19  Women are more superstitious/more sentimental.

20  **miracles are sought**  Saints' relics were thought to have miraculous powers.

21  **I . . . taught**  I wish to have that future age taught by this poem . . .

23–6  Their love was truly platonic.

27  **coming and going**  It was the normal custom to kiss both on meeting and on leaving a friend.

28  **not between those meals**  They controlled their sexual appetites.

29–30  In nature there are no restrictions ('seals') on sexual activity, but since the Fall in the Garden of Eden, when Adam and Eve clothed their nakedness, man has known shame and has imposed subsequent ('late') laws to control his desires. The lovers have observed these laws.

31  Platonic love is the true miracle.

32  **measure**  limits (perhaps of metrical scansion).
    **pass**  go beyond (surpass).

# Song

Sweetest love, I do not go,
   For weariness of thee,
Nor in hope the world can show
   A fitter love for me;
     But since that I                5
Must die at last, 'tis best,
To use my self in jest
   Thus by feigned deaths to die.

Yesternight the sun went hence,
   And yet is here today;             10
He hath no desire nor sense,
   Nor half so short a way:
     Then fear not me,
But believe that I shall make
Speedier journeys, since I take         15
   More wings and spurs than he.

O how feeble is man's power,
   That if good fortune fall,
Cannot add another hour,
   Nor a lost hour recall!         20
     But come bad chance,
And we join to it our strength,
And we teach it art and length,
   Itself o'er us to advance.

When thou sigh'st, thou sigh'st not wind,   25
   But sigh'st my soul away,

When thou weep'st, unkindly kind,
  My life's blood doth decay.
    It cannot be
That thou lov'st me, as thou say'st,          30
If in thine my life thou waste;
  Thou art the best of me.

Let not thy divining heart
  Forethink me any ill,
Destiny may take thy part,          35
  And may thy fears fulfil;
    But think that we
Are but turned aside to sleep;
They who one another keep
  Alive, ne'er parted be.          40

5–8  They will inevitably be separated when he dies and so it is best to prepare for this by his earlier absences which are 'feigned deaths'.

16  **wings and spurs** The incentive of his love makes him travel more speedily than the sun which has no 'desire' (line 11).

18  **fall** occur (befall).

20  **a lost hour** i.e. of good fortune.

23–4  **And . . . advance** We teach misfortune cunning ways to prolong itself and to dominate us.

25–32  The pair are so united in love that they are each other and so *her* distress causes *his* spiritual and physical decay.

33  **divining** conjecturing.

34  **Forethink . . . ill** anticipate misfortune happening to me.

35–6  Destiny may take her side by bringing misfortune on the poet, thus fulfilling her nervous fears.

38  **but** only; their separation is no more than a sleep.

39–40  Since they possess each other's hearts they can never truly be parted. Compare this with the treatment of the same theme in 'A Valediction: forbidding Mourning' (p51) which Walton thought was written at the same time before Donne left his wife on a journey to the Continent in 1611.

# The Sun Rising

       Busy old fool, unruly sun,
       Why dost thou thus,
Through windows, and through curtains call on us?
Must to thy motions lovers' seasons run?
        Saucy pedantic wretch, go chide          5
        Late school-boys, and sour prentices,
  Go tell court-huntsmen, that the King will ride,
  Call country ants to harvest offices;
Love, all alike, no season knows, nor clime,
Nor hours, days, months, which are the rags of time.    10

       Thy beams, so reverend, and strong
       Why shouldst thou think?
I could eclipse and cloud them with a wink,
But that I would not lose her sight so long:
        If her eyes have not blinded thine,       15
        Look, and tomorrow late, tell me,
  Whether both the Indias of spice and mine
  Be where thou left'st them, or lie here with me.
Ask for those kings whom thou saw'st yesterday,
And thou shalt hear, All here in one bed lay.    20

       She is all states, and all princes, I,
       Nothing else is.
Princes do but play us; compared to this,
All honour's mimic; all wealth alchemy.
        Thou sun art half as happy as we,      25
        In that the world's contracted thus;
  Thine age asks ease, and since thy duties be
  To warm the world, that's done in warming us.
Shine here to us, and thou art everywhere;
This bed thy centre is, these walls, thy sphere.    30

The *aubade* or dawn song is a traditional type of love poem; see
Ovid's treatment of it in Marlowe's translation of *Elegies* I, 13
(p161), but Donne's approach is vigorously original.

1 **Busy** interfering (as in busybody).
  **unruly** unmanageable, ill-mannered.

4 **Must . . . run** Must lovers be subject to earthly considerations of time dictated by the sun's motions? The implication, as in lines 9 and 10, is that their love is on a heavenly plane.

5 **pedantic** irritatingly precise (like a schoolmaster).

6 **prentices** apprentices.

7 **court-huntsmen** courtiers who go on an early-morning hunt with James I and VI, perhaps because they are 'hunting' for advancement at court.

8 **country ants** the townsman's contemptuous term for busy farm workers.
**offices** tasks.

9 **Love . . . clime** Love, which is always unchanging, takes no notice of time and place.

10 **rags of time** the periods into which time can be separated (the outward trappings of time are insignificant to a love that is timeless).

11–12 inverted word order; the question is a comic attack on the sun's supposed self-importance.

13 **wink** closing both eyes.

15 Her eyes are so bright that they will dazzle the sun!

17–18 Not only is the whole world contracted into his mistress, but she is sweetly perfumed (the spices of the East Indies) and his treasure (the gold mines of the West Indies).

22 Nothing exists apart from their love.

23–4 Since their love is the one reality everything else is mere imitation or illusion. One aim of alchemy was to turn base metal into gold, but since it was discredited by then it is used here for something impressive but false.

30 The bed is the earth about which the sun is to revolve and so the walls of the bedroom will be its orbit.


# The Triple Fool

I am two fools, I know,
For loving, and for saying so
    In whining poetry;

But where's that wiseman, that would not be I,
  If she would not deny?                                        5
Then as the earth's inward narrow crooked lanes
Do purge sea water's fretful salt away,
  I thought, if I could draw my pains
Through rhyme's vexation, I should them allay.
Grief brought to numbers cannot be so fierce,                   10
For, he tames it, that fetters it in verse.

  But when I have done so,
Some man, his art and voice to show,
  Doth set and sing my pain,
And, by delighting many, frees again                            15
  Grief, which verse did restrain.
To love and grief tribute of verse belongs,
But not of such as pleases when 'tis read;
  Both are increasèd by such songs:
For both their triumphs so are publishèd,                       20
And I, which was two fools, do so grow three;
Who are a little wise, the best fools be.

4–5 **But . . . deny** But who is so wise that they would not wish to take my
     place if only she would not reject me?

6–9 Just as sea water loses its salt when it is drawn through 'earth's
     inward narrow crooked lanes' into a fresh river, so his suffering
     would be reduced ('allayed') if drawn into the 'narrow' restriction
     ('vexation') of an elaborate verse form. (The *salt* tears would be
     filtered out.)

  10 **numbers** poetry (in particular its metre).

  13 **art** skill.

  14 **set** set to music; this happened to a number of Donne's poems.

15–16 Paradoxically delight in the music sets free the grief which had been
     'fettered' by the verse form.

  17 **To . . . belongs** Love and grief should have a tribute of verse.

  18 **such** i.e. such verse.

21–2 He was 'a little wise' in easing his pain by writing poetry, but
     paradoxically now that his songs are performed his pain is intensified
     making him a fool a third time now, one of the 'best fools'.

# Twicknam Garden

Blasted with sighs, and surrounded with tears,
    Hither I come to seek the spring,
    And at mine eyes, and at mine ears,
Receive such balms, as else cure everything;
    But O, self traitor, I do bring                               5
The spider love, which transubstantiates all,
    And can convert manna to gall,
And that this place may thoroughly be thought
    True paradise, I have the serpent brought.

'Twere wholesomer for me, that winter did                        10
    Benight the glory of this place,
    And that a grave frost did forbid
These trees to laugh, and mock me to my face;
    But that I may not this disgrace
Endure, nor yet leave loving, Love, let me                       15
    Some senseless piece of this place be;
Make me a mandrake, so I may groan here,
    Or a stone fountain weeping out my year.

Hither with crystal vials, lovers come,
    And take my tears, which are love's wine,                    20
    And try your mistress' tears at home,
For all are false, that taste not just like mine;
    Alas, hearts do not in eyes shine,
Nor can you more judge woman's thoughts by tears,
    Than by her shadow, what she wears.                          25
O perverse sex, where none is true but she,
    Who's therefore true, because her truth kills me.

Twickenham Park was the home of Donne's patroness, the Countess
of Bedford. The poem follows Petrarchan convention (the poet
disappointed in love seeks comfort unavailingly from nature), but the
treatment is original (see introduction, p6).

4  **balms** the scents of a spring garden, but also soothing medicines.
   **else** otherwise.

6–7  A closely knit series of images shows his love to be the reverse of divine love. His love is spider-like (turning all that it eats to poison), whereas divine love changes (through transubstantiation) the bread and wine of the mass into the body and blood of Christ, whose death on the cross is the supreme example of unselfish love. 'Manna' was food from heaven given to the Jews during the Exodus and a type (or foreshadowing) of the bread of the mass or communion and here is turned into bitter 'gall' or poison.

9 **the serpent** not just evil temptation (as in the story of Adam and Eve) but more specifically envy.

10 **that** if.
**winter** It is spring (line 2).

14 **that** in order that.

15 **leave** stop.

16 **senseless** lacking the ability to feel or move; if he becomes a mandrake or weeping fountain he will not 'leave loving' and yet will no longer feel shame.

17 **mandrake** Its forked root was thought to resemble a man and it was supposed to 'groan' when pulled from the ground.

19–20 Lovers will visit the fountain to collect his tears (just as pilgrims visiting a shrine take away bottles of holy water; e.g. at Lourdes or Walsingham). The fountain is the shrine of a martyr to love.

21 **try** test.

23 **Alas . . . shine** You cannot find out someone's true feelings just by looking them in the eyes.

26–7 The perversity lies in the fact that the only woman who is loyal ('true') is loyal to another solely in order to torment the poet.

# A Valediction: forbidding Mourning

As virtuous men pass mildly away,
  And whisper to their souls, to go,
Whilst some of their sad friends do say,
  The breath goes now, and some say, no:

So let us melt, and make no noise,
  No tear-floods, nor sigh-tempests move,

5

'Twere profanation of our joys
   To tell the laity our love.

Moving of the earth brings harms and fears,
   Men reckon what it did and meant,          10
But trepidation of the spheres,
   Though greater far, is innocent.

Dull sublunary lovers' love
   (Whose soul is sense) cannot admit
Absence, because it doth remove          15
   Those things which elemented it.

But we by a love, so much refined,
   That our selves know not what it is,
Inter-assurèd of the mind,
   Care less, eyes, lips, and hands to miss.     20

Our two souls therefore, which are one,
   Though I must go, endure not yet
A breach, but an expansïon,
   Like gold to aery thinness beat.

If they be two, they are two so          25
   As stiff twin compasses are two,
Thy soul the fixed foot, makes no show
   To move, but doth, if the other do.

And though it in the centre sit,
   Yet when the other far doth roam,     30
It leans, and hearkens after it,
   And grows erect, as that comes home.

Such wilt thou be to me, who must
   Like the other foot, obliquely run;
Thy firmness makes my circle just,     35
   And makes me end, where I begun.

**Valediction** farewell; a common type of love poem.

1–5  An extended simile: Just as no-one is certain of the precise moment
      at which a man with a clear conscience slips away from this life, so
      let us part unobtrusively.

6  Compare the opening of 'Twicknam Garden' (p50).

7–8 It would be a desecration ('profanation') of the sacred mystery of their love to reveal it to ordinary people ('laity' = those who are not priests).

9 **harms and fears** Earthquakes are not only destructive, but also bad omens.

11 In the old cosmology the movements of the heavenly bodies were accounted for by the revolution of a series of concentric crystal spheres about the earth. This theory did not account for the precession of the equinoxes which was explained away by a movement ('trepidation') of one of the outer spheres.

12 **innocent** harmless.

13 **sublunary** Everything below the innermost sphere, that of the moon, was thought to be subject to change and decay; everything above it was thought to be changeless and eternal. Donne and his mistress are, by implication, far above the sphere of the moon and so their separation is, like the 'trepidation of the spheres', harmless.

14 **sense** the senses.
**admit** tolerate.

16 Their love is given existence ('elemented') by the presence of each other's physical charms.

17–18 For the idea of a love that refines and is indefinable see 'The Ecstasy', lines 25–32 (p34).

19–20 Mutually confident of their platonic love they are unconcerned by the beloved's physical absence.

22–4 Their 'refined' love is like pure gold which is spread out over a wide area without being broken when hammered into gold leaf.
**aery** not simply airy, but also of the spirit as opposed to bodily.

27 **fixed** not merely on the paper, but in her faithful love. The 'fixed foot' does not appear to move, but rotates in response to the movement of the outer half.

31 **hearkens after** seeks for news of; this and the erotic hint of the next line give life to the image.

34 **obliquely** indirectly (i.e. in a curve), but there is a hint of unfaithfulness which is countered by 'firmness' and 'just'.

35 **firmness** two meanings as for 'fixed'.
**just** The completed circle is a symbol of endless perfection.

36 **where I begun** with his beloved; although the analogy is closely argued it is, of course, in one sense illogical since the distance between the legs of the compasses remains constant.

# Woman's Constancy

Now thou hast loved me one whole day,
Tomorrow when thou leav'st, what wilt thou say?
Wilt thou then antedate some new made vow?
        Or say that now
We are not just those persons, which we were?      5
Or, that oaths made in reverential fear
Of Love, and his wrath, any may forswear?
Or, as true deaths, true marriages untie,
So lovers' contracts, images of those,
Bind but till sleep, death's image, them unloose?      10
        Or, your own end to justify,
For having purposed change, and falsehood, you
Can have no way but falsehood to be true?
Vain lunatic, against these 'scapes I could
        Dispute, and conquer, if I would,      15
        Which I abstain to do,
For by tomorrow, I may think so too.

3  **antedate** claim that 'some new made vow' was made *before* her vow to him and so has priority.

5  **We are not just those persons** We are not exactly the same as we were (and so the vows no longer apply).

6–7  **that . . . forswear** Anyone may break an oath made under duress for fear of Love's anger.

8–10  **as . . . unloose** Sleep is an image of death and lovers' vows are an image of marriage vows; therefore lovers' vows are terminated by sleep as marriage vows are by death.

12–13  Since she has resolved on ('purposed') change, paradoxically she can only be true to herself by being false.

14  **'scapes** evasive arguments.

15  **if I would** if I wished.

17  **think so too** wish to be inconstant as well.

# Elegy 7

Nature's lay idiot, I taught thee to love,
And in that sophistry, oh, thou dost prove
Too subtle: Fool, thou didst not understand
The mystic language of the eye nor hand:
Nor couldst thou judge the difference of the air          5
Of sighs, and say, this lies, this sounds despair:
Nor by the eye's water call a malady
Desperately hot, or changing feverously.
I had not taught thee then, the alphabet
Of flowers, how they devisefully being set          10
And bound up, might with speechless secrecy
Deliver errands mutely, and mutually.
Remember since all thy words used to be
To every suitor, *Ay, if my friends agree*;
Since, household charms, thy husband's name to teach,          15
Were all the love-tricks, that thy wit could reach;
And since, an hour's discourse could scarce have made
One answer in thee, and that ill arrayed
In broken proverbs, and torn sentences.
Thou art not by so many duties his,          20
That from the world's common having severed thee,
Inlaid thee, neither to be seen, nor see,
As mine: who have with amorous delicacies
Refined thee into a blissful paradise.
Thy graces and good words my creatures be;          25
I planted knowledge and life's tree in thee,
Which oh, shall strangers taste? Must I alas
Frame and enamel plate, and drink in glass?
Chafe wax for others' seals? break a colt's force
And leave him then, being made a ready horse?          30

1 **lay** uninitiated in the mysteries of love.
2 **sophistry** art of deception.
6 **sounds** reveals by its sound.
7 **the eyes' water** tears used by the experienced lover to diagnose the emotional 'malady' (disease) of another lover, as a doctor diagnoses disease by examining the 'water' (urine) of a patient.

10 **devisefully** as a code.

12 **errands** messages between the lovers.

13 **since** when (i.e. the time before she had been taught to love).

15 **household charms** homely spells used by girls to find the names of their future husbands.

17 **since** see line 13.

17–19 She used to have little to say for herself in polite conversation ('discourse') and what she did say was poorly expressed ('ill arrayed') in old proverbs and commonplace maxims ('sentences').

21 **That . . . thee** Who prevented you from being possessed by anyone but himself; i.e. her husband. The image is of enclosing common land for private fields, but the poet feels that she should be *his* 'paradise' instead (line 24).

22 **Inlaid thee** hid you away.

25–7 Her good qualities were the creation ('creatures') of the poet in his paradise who also gave her sexual knowledge just as God created the Garden of Eden and planted the trees of the knowledge of good and evil and of life. If any other man enjoys her it will be a sin comparable to Eve's 'tasting' of the apple.

28 He has made her very attractive (made a goblet of gold or silver and decorated it with enamel) and must he now settle for some less attractive woman (drink from a plain glass)?

29 **Chafe wax for others' seals** Soften the wax by rubbing and warming it so that other men may stamp their seal upon it. Both 'wax' and 'colt' are images of the woman that he trains in the art of love only to find that others seize the advantage.

# Four Epigrams

*Hero and Leander*
Both robbed of air, we both lie in one ground,
Both whom one fire had burnt, one water drowned.

*Pyramus and Thisbe*
Two, by themselves, each other, love and fear
Slain, cruel friends, by parting have joined here.

A *Lame Beggar*
I am unable, yonder beggar cries,                        5
To stand, or move; if he say true, he *lies*.

*Disinherited*
Thy father all from thee, by his last will,
Gave to the poor; thou hast good title still.

**Epigrams** were imitated from the short, witty verses of classical
poets and especially Martial (see Fanshawe's translation on p165). In
Donne's epigrams we see in isolation the terse wit that he uses so
effectively in his longer poems.

**Hero and Leander** Leander was drowned when swimming the
Hellespont to visit Hero whom he loved; she drowned herself in
despair. Each of the four elements – *air, ground, fire* and *water* – is
mentioned. The 'one fire' is their mutual love.

**Pyramus and Thisbe** Separated by their parents these lovers planned
to run away together. Thisbe hid from a lion and Pyramus, believing
her to be dead, committed suicide. Thisbe returned and committed
suicide beside her dying lover. Paradoxically 'parting' the lovers has
caused them to be 'joined' in death.

8  **title** an entitlement to claim his inheritance since, being disinherited,
he is now poor.

# Satire 3

Kind pity chokes my spleen; brave scorn forbids
Those tears to issue which swell my eye-lids;
I must not laugh, nor weep sins, and be wise;
Can railing then cure these worn maladies?
Is not our mistress fair religiön,                       5
As worthy of all our soul's devotiön,
As virtue was to the first blinded age?
Are not heaven's joys as valiant to assuage
Lusts, as earth's honour was to them? Alas,
As we do them in means, shall they surpass              10
Us in the end, and shall thy father's spirit

Meet blind philosophers in heaven, whose merit
Of strict life may be imputed faith, and hear
Thee, whom he taught so easy ways and near
To follow, damned? O if thou dar'st, fear this;                    15
This fear great courage, and high valour is.
Dar'st thou aid mutinous Dutch, and dar'st thou lay
Thee in ships' wooden sepulchres, a prey
To leaders' rage, to storms, to shot, to dearth?
Dar'st thou dive seas, and dungeons of the earth?                  20
Hast thou courageous fire to thaw the ice
Of frozen north discoveries? and thrice
Colder than salamanders, like divine
Children in the oven, fires of Spain, and the line,
Whose countries limbecks to our bodies be,                         25
Canst thou for gain bear? and must every he
Which cries not, 'Goddess!' to thy mistress, draw,
Or eat thy poisonous words? courage of straw!
O desperate coward, wilt thou seem bold, and
To thy foes and his (who made thee to stand                        30
Sentinel in his world's garrison) thus yield,
And for forbidden wars, leave the appointed field?
Know thy foes: the foul Devil, he, whom thou
Strivest to please, for hate, not love, would allow
Thee fain, his whole realm to be quit; and as                      35
The world's all parts wither away and pass,
So the world's self, thy other loved foe, is
In her decrepit wane, and thou loving this,
Dost love a withered and worn strumpet; last,
Flesh (itself's death) and joys which flesh can taste,             40
Thou lovest; and thy fair goodly soul, which doth
Give this flesh power to taste joy, thou dost loathe.
    Seek true religiön. O where? Mirreus
Thinking her unhoused here, and fled from us,
Seeks her at Rome, there, because he doth know                     45
That she was there a thousand years ago;
He loves her rags so, as we here obey
The statecloth where the Prince sat yesterday.
Crantz to such brave loves will not be enthralled,

But loves her only, who at Geneva is called                    50
Religiön, plain, simple, sullen, young,
Contemptuous, yet unhandsome; as among
Lecherous humours, there is one that judges
No wenches wholesome, but coarse country drudges.
Graius stays still at home here, and because                   55
Some preachers, vile ambitious bawds, and laws
Still new like fashions, bid him think that she
Which dwells with us, is only perfect, he
Embraceth her, whom his godfathers will
Tender to him, being tender, as wards still                    60
Take such wives as their guardians offer, or
Pay values. Careless Phrygius doth abhor
All, because all cannot be good, as one
Knowing some women whores, dares marry none.
Gracchus loves all as one, and thinks that so                  65
As women do in divers countries go
In divers habits, yet are still one kind,
So doth, so is religion; and this blind-
ness too much light breeds; but unmovèd thou
Of force must one, and forced but one allow;                   70
And the right; ask thy father which is she,
Let him ask his; though truth and falsehood be
Near twins, yet truth a little elder is;
Be busy to seek her, believe me this,
He's not of none, nor worst, that seeks the best.              75
To adore, or scorn an image, or protest,
May all be bad; doubt wisely, in strange way
To stand inquiring right, is not to stray;
To sleep, or run wrong is. On a huge hill,
Craggèd, and steep, Truth stands, and he that will             80
Reach her, about must, and about must go,
And what the hill's suddenness resists, win so;
Yet strive so, that before age, death's twilight,
Thy soul rest, for none can work in that night;
To will, implies delay, therefore now do.                      85
Hard deeds, the body's pains; hard knowledge too
The mind's endeavours reach, and mysteries

Are like the sun, dazzling, yet plain to all eyes.
Keep the truth which thou hast found; men do not stand
In so ill case here, that God hath with his hand                    90
Signed kings blank-charters to kill whom they hate,
Nor are they vicars, but hangmen to Fate.
Fool and wretch, wilt thou let thy soul be tied
To man's laws, by which she shall not be tried
At the last day? Or will it then boot thee                          95
To say a Philip, or a Gregory,
A Harry, or a Martin taught thee this?
Is not this excuse for mere contraries,
Equally strong; cannot both sides say so?
That thou mayst rightly obey power, her bounds know;    100
Those past, her nature, and name is changed; to be
Then humble to her is idolatry;
As streams are, power is; those blest flowers that dwell
At the rough stream's calm head, thrive and prove well,
But having left their roots, and themselves given           105
To the stream's tyrannous rage, alas are driven
Through mills, and rocks, and woods, and at last, almost
Consumed in going, in the sea are lost:
So perish souls, which more choose men's unjust
Power from God claimed, than God himself to trust.    110

This poem is given its very distinctive quality by the poet's fierce
insistence that truth can, and must, be found. This insistence derives
from the fact that the poem was written at a time (between 1593 and
1598) when Donne was moving towards the Church of England and
away from the deeply committed faith of his Roman Catholic family.
(He was descended through his mother from Thomas More; two of
his uncles were Jesuits; and his brother died of fever while in
Newgate for harbouring a Catholic priest.) The struggle is revealed
in a certain inconsistency, for when he talks in line 14 of 'easy ways
and near' to salvation he echoes the reassuring Catholic approach
which made it possible to earn salvation by doing good deeds. These
'easy ways' are obviously opposed to the 'hard knowledge' of line 86
which suggests that man must depend on himself and God and not
on an intermediary body such as the Church of Rome claimed to be.
The mood at the end of the poem seems one of Protestantism, but
not of final commitment.

1 **spleen** the bodily organ supposedly responsible for causing laughter
and ridicule; as Donne considers man's folly his emotions of
contempt and sympathy are in conflict.

3 **and be wise** Wisdom is incompatible with either laughter ('scorn') or
weeping ('pity').

4 **railing** abusing, criticising.

5–15 **Is not . . . damned** Are we not to show as much loyalty to
Christianity as the pagans (the Greeks and Romans who were 'blind'
because they came before Christ) show to Virtue? Is the hope of
heavenly bliss not as powerful ('valiant') in controlling our sinful
desires as the hope of earthly honour was for the pagans. Alas,
although we have the better way ('means') of getting to heaven, are
they going to get the better of us in reaching that target ('end'). Will
your father's soul meet pre-Christian pagan moralists in heaven
whose strictly virtuous lives will be accepted as making up for the
faith that they could not have ('imputed faith' = attributed to them
as faith), while he hears that you, his Christian son, whom he taught
to follow the easy and direct ('near') path to heaven, have been
damned? Although Donne is here addressing the reader in the second
person ('thy', 'thee') the poem may also be read as being addressed to
himself.

16 Paradoxically the acceptance of the fear of damnation implies
spiritual courage.

17 **mutinous Dutch** Dutch Protestants who were rebelling against their
Catholic Spanish conquerors.

18 **ships' wooden sepulchres** Life on board is so hazardous that the ship
is compared to a wooden coffin.
**prey** victim.

19 **dearth** scarcity of food.

22 **frozen north discoveries** There were attempts at this time to discover
a north-west passage to the Pacific.

23 **salamanders** lizard-like creatures supposedly so cold that they
quenched the heat of the fire in which they lived.

24 **Children in the oven** Shadrach, Meshach and Abednego were
thrown into 'the burning fiery furnace' on the orders of King
Nebuchadnezzar, but they were not burnt (Daniel 3.19–30).
**fires of Spain** a reference to the Spanish Inquisition.
**the line** the equator.

25 **limbecks** Because of their heat equatorial countries are compared to alembics (early types of retort used for distilling).

26 **Canst thou for gain bear?** Can you endure all these hardships (which the poet has just listed) for material (as opposed to spiritual) gain?

26–8 **must . . . straw** Must every man who does not address your mistress as 'Goddess!' either draw his sword to defend himself or swallow your insults? Such courage is a sham (by comparison with the true courage of lines 15–16).

30 **his** God's.

32 **And . . . fight** And will you leave the spiritual battlefield where God has told you to fight ('the appointed field') to fight in forbidden worldly battles?

33–5 **the foul . . . quit** The foul Devil (whom you try to please) would, from motives of hate, not love, willingly ('fain') allow you to have his whole kingdom (Hell) in order to be rid of it.

36 **world's all parts** all the things of this world.

37 **thy other loved foe** another paradox; the newly baptised Christian promises to renounce the devil, the world and the flesh (i.e. the three 'foes' which Donne is examining here), but although failure to renounce them will lead to damnation Donne finds them attractive.

38 **her decrepit wane** The world was thought to be decaying and near its end.

39 **strumpet** prostitute.

40 **Flesh (itself's death)** The body is the cause of its own death. The 'joys which flesh can taste', or the 'carnal desires of the flesh' in the words of the baptism service in *The Book of Common Prayer*, lead to sin and so to death. (For the link between sin and death read Genesis 3.)

41–2 The soul animates the body.

43 **Mirreus** Myrrheus, the myrrh-scented man; not a particular man but a typical Roman Catholic using incense for worship.

47 **rags** the tattered remnants of Christian truth and perhaps also, satirically, the rich and elaborate vestments worn by Roman Catholic priests (cf. 'brave' in line 49).

48 **statecloth** canopy over the throne; it was customary to bow to the throne even when it was empty.

49 **Crantz** a Dutch name suggestive of a Protestant.
**brave** ostentatiously dressed.
**enthralled** enslaved.

50 **Geneva** the home of Calvinism, the form of Protestantism most strongly opposed to the Roman Catholic church.

53 **Lecherous humours** those who have a taste for lechery.

55 **Graius** literally a Greek; 'Greek' was a term sometimes used for a trickster or cheat and perhaps implies intellectual dishonesty in accepting the doctrines of the Church of England unquestioningly.

56 **ambitious bawds** The implication is that Church of England clergymen recommend their form of Christianity to advance themselves in the world just as a 'bawd' or pimp recommends a girl's attractions in order to make money.
**laws** recent laws designed to enforce religious conformity.

58 **only** alone.

59 **godfathers** At baptism godparents renounce sin and make a profession of faith on behalf of the infant who cannot speak or think for himself.

60 **Tender to him** offer him.
**tender** young and easily influenced.

62 **Pay values** A ward who refused to marry the woman chosen for him by his guardian had to pay a fine ('Pay values') as did anyone who refused to attend his parish church.
**Phrygius** A Phrygian; this term is used in writings of the period to describe the supporters of Montanism, a form of heresy. Perhaps its use here implies a condemnation of Phrygius's attitude.

65 **Gracchus** a broad-minded person? The Gracchi were a Roman family with a 'tradition of democracy and independence' (H. H. Scullard, *From the Gracchi to Nero*. London, 1959).
**as one** equally.

66 **divers** various (diverse).

67 **habits** costumes.
**one kind** i.e. they are all women.

68–9 **this blind-/ness** an excess of light (i.e. assuming that everyone has the light of truth) causes ('breeds') a blindness (to the only religious truth that there is).

69–70 **but . . . allow** Whether you are left to make up your own mind ('unmoved' by others) or whether you are put under pressure ('forced') you must of necessity ('of force') choose one and only ('but') one.

71 **And the right** The right choice is vital. The torments of hell (the

punishment for the wrong choice) were horrifyingly real to Donne and his contemporaries. He later came to accept that all Christian churches might show the way to salvation, but his attitude was inconsistent; see note to lines 101–2.

**ask thy father which is she** Donne echoes a passage in Deuteronomy in which the Jews are urged to return to the true religion of their forefathers: 'ask thy father, and he will shew thee; Thy elders and they will tell thee' (Deuteronomy 32.7).

75–7 **He's not . . . bad** The man who is actively seeking the best church (and who is therefore not closely attached to any church) should not be thought of as having no religion or an inferior one. To be a Roman Catholic ('To adore . . . an image'), to scorn Catholic rituals ('scorn an image') and to be a Protestant ('to protest') may all be wrong.

77 **doubt wisely** The lines which follow make it clear that this is not passive advice, but involves a most strenuous search for truth.

77–9 **in strange . . . wrong is** To stop and ask the way on an unfamiliar road ('in strange way') is to avoid going wrong, but to make no effort ('sleep') or to set off without being sure of the way is to go wrong.

79–82 The image is of a hill's steepness ('suddenness') which can only be overcome by the climber who is prepared to toil, zigzagging his way to the top ('about . . . and about').

84 **night** death.

85 **To will . . . do** To have good intentions ('To will') implies that you are delaying; therefore get to work immediately.

86–7 **Hard deeds . . . reach** Difficult actions require physical exertion and difficult knowledge requires mental exertion.

87–8 **mysteries . . . eyes** Religious mysteries may be difficult to grasp and yet their truth is apparent to all (just as the sun is obviously there even if too 'dazzling' to look at). The associations of the sun image are complex (light = life and goodness; kingship; Jesus who is the light of the world and the *Son* of God who *rose* from the dead), but here it is clearly set against the image of 'night' (line 84) with its suggestion of confusion as well as death.

90 **In so ill case** in such a desperate situation.

91 **blank-charters** a signed execution warrant with a space left for the victim's name to be filled in. Kings are not given *carte blanche* by God to do whatever they like.

92   **Nor . . . Fate** Kings are not Fate's deputies ('vicars'), but merely the means by which Fate's decrees are fulfilled.

95   **At the last day?** the day of judgement when your soul will be tried by God's laws and not man's.
   **boot thee** help you.

96   **Philip** Philip II of Spain, the champion of the Roman Catholic Counter-Reformation. He was married to the Catholic Mary I of England (Elizabeth I's half-sister and predecessor). He made use of the Inquisition in trying to control his rebellious Dutch subjects and was responsible for the Armada (1588) not long before this poem was written.
   **Gregory** There are plenty to choose from! Perhaps Donne has in mind the Pope of his childhood, Gregory XIII, who worked with Philip II to resist the Protestant reformation, or Gregory VII who had excommunicated and deposed the Holy Roman Emperor Henry IV. (The excommunication of Elizabeth I in 1570 legitimised Catholic plots against her life.)

97   **Harry** Henry VIII; not a whole-hearted Protestant, but responsible for England's break with the Church of Rome.
   **Martin** Martin Luther, an Augustinian monk and professor of theology, was the first great inspirer of the Reformation. One of his principal theories was that of 'justification by faith' and not just by good deeds as Roman Catholics argued (see introduction to poem, p60).

98–9   This excuse (i.e. hiding behind the authority of one of the leaders named in the previous two lines) is equally convincing (or rather by implication unconvincing) for people whose beliefs are completely opposed ('mere' means absolute or downright).

100   **bounds** the limits of secular authority. For the basis of Christian teaching on this see Luke 20.21–6.

101–2   **Those past . . . idolatry** Power becomes tyranny once it goes beyond those limits. To obey the state in matters of religion is to make an idol of the state. Later in life Donne was to speak in favour of those laws which compelled religious conformity, but his attitude was inconsistent (see note to line 71). Since he was a convert from a devout Roman Catholic family who had risen to be Dean of St Paul's by a combination of determined canvassing and royal patronage his inconsistency is not surprising.

103–10   **those blest . . . trust** Earthly power ('the rough stream') originates from God (the 'calm head' or spring) and those souls ('blest flowers') that devote themselves to God ('that dwell/At the rough stream's calm head') flourish, but those that trust earthly power (that are further down the river) are destroyed by that power ('given/To the stream's tyrannous rage' and 'lost').

# Divine Meditations

4
Oh my black soul! now thou art summonèd
By sickness, death's herald, and champiön;
Thou art like a pilgrim, which abroad hath done
Treason, and durst not turn to whence he is fled,
Or like a thief, which till death's doom be read,                    5
Wisheth himself delivered from prison;
But damned and haled to executiön,
Wisheth that still he might be imprisonèd;
Yet grace, if thou repent, thou canst not lack;
But who shall give thee that grace to begin?                    10
Oh make thyself with holy mourning black,
And red with blushing, as thou art with sin;
Or wash thee in Christ's blood, which hath this might
That being red, it dyes red souls to white.

 1   **black**  with sin.

1–2  **summonèd By sickness**  Sickness is a summoner to God's court because it leads to death which is followed by judgement.

 4   He dares not return to the place from which he has fled.

 5   **death's doom**  the death sentence.

 7   **haled**  dragged.

9–10  God's grace (the unearned gift of God's favour) is freely available as long as the sinner chooses to repent and to accept it, but the poet needs grace in order to repent in the first place.

 11  **black**  no longer with sin (line 1), but in mourning repentance for sin.

 12  **red**  blushing with shame for his sins which are also 'red' (most wicked). Compare 'though your sins be as scarlet, they shall be as white as snow; though they be red like crimson, they shall be as wool (Isaiah 1.18).

13 **might** power.

14 **dyes** Sin *dies* and the soul is *dyed* a new colour being washed free of
sin. The redeemed in heaven are described as those who 'have
washed their robes, and made them white in the blood of the Lamb'
(Revelation 7.14).


7
At the round earth's imagined corners, blow
Your trumpets, angels, and arise, arise
From death, you numberless infinities
Of souls, and to your scattered bodies go,
All whom the flood did, and fire shall o'erthrow,                    5
All whom war, dearth, age, agues, tyrannies,
Despair, law, chance, hath slain, and you whose eyes
Shall behold God, and never taste death's woe.
But let them sleep, Lord, and me mourn a space,
For, if above all these, my sins abound,                            10
'Tis late to ask abundance of thy grace,
When we are there; here on this lowly ground,
Teach me how to repent; for that's as good
As if thou hadst sealed my pardon, with thy blood.

In Revelation St John the Divine gives a visionary account of the end
of the world in which each new disaster is heralded by an angel
blowing a trumpet. It is preceded by an account of those who are
saved beginning: 'I saw four angels standing on the four corners of
the earth'. (7.1). The 'corners' are not merely 'imagined' in the sense
of being unreal, but as part of a spiritual exercise (imagining the end
of the world) which leads to the repentance expressed in the
contrastingly subdued sestet.

4 **scattered bodies** Souls return to their bodies for the resurrection of
the dead.
5 **All . . . o'erthrow** all who have been and will be killed in the course
of history from Noah's flood to the fires that will end the world (see
for example Revelation 8 and 9).
7–8 **you whose eyes . . .** those still living at the end of the world who will
therefore find themselves face to face with God without experiencing

death. 'We shall not all sleep [i.e. die], but we shall all be changed, In a moment, in the twinkling of an eye, at the last trump' (I Corinthians 15.51–2).

11  **grace** forgiving favour.

12  **there** before the judgement throne.
    **this lowly ground** earth.

14  **sealed** confirmed; Christ's death saves man from sin and his blood is like the wax stamped with an official seal to authorise a pardon. See again Revelation 7.3 in which the 'servants of God' are 'sealed . . . in their foreheads'.

## 10

Death be not proud, though some have callèd thee
Mighty and dreadful, for, thou art not so,
For, those, whom thou think'st, thou dost overthrow,
Die not, poor death, nor yet canst thou kill me;
From rest and sleep, which but thy pictures be,                5
Much pleasure, then from thee, much more must flow,
And soonest our best men with thee do go,
Rest of their bones, and soul's delivery.
Thou art slave to fate, chance, kings, and desperate men,
And dost with poison, war, and sickness dwell,              10
And poppy, or charms can make us sleep as well,
And better than thy stroke; why swell'st thou then?
One short sleep past, we wake eternally,
And death shall be no more, Death thou shalt die.

4  To the Christian, death is merely the gateway to eternal life.

5–6  Since 'rest and sleep', which are only ('but') images of death, give 'Much pleasure', death itself will give still more.

7  **And soonest . . . go** 'The virtuous die young', or more probably, 'the virtuous are happy to die'.

8  Death gives rest to their bodies and sets free their souls; there is a suggestion of re-birth in 'delivery'.

9–12  Death is asked contemptuously why it swells with pride since it is a 'slave', keeps bad company, and is no more effective than a sleeping drug ('poppy') or spell.

13 **we wake eternally** we wake from death to eternal life.

14 See again I Corinthians 15, especially verse 26: 'The last enemy that shall be destroyed is death.'

14
Batter my heart, three-personed God; for, you
As yet but knock, breathe, shine, and seek to mend;
That I may rise, and stand, o'erthrow me, and bend
Your force, to break, blow, burn, and make me new.
I, like an usurped town, to another due,                                    5
Labour to admit you, but oh, to no end,
Reason your viceroy in me, me should defend,
But is captived, and proves weak or untrue,
Yet dearly I love you, and would be lovèd fain,
But am betrothed unto your enemy;                                          10
Divorce me, untie, or break that knot again,
Take me to you, imprison me, for I
Except you enthral me, never shall be free,
Nor ever chaste, except you ravish me.

1 **Batter** The forceful opening is appropriate both for the image of the blacksmith hammering on the anvil and for the siege images which follow.

  **three-personed God** God in all three aspects of the Trinity: Father, Son and Holy Ghost.

3 Paradoxically he can only truly stand after he has been 'o'erthrown' and conquered by God.

4 Each verb here is a stronger counterpart of those in line 2; the poet is like an object which is past repair and must be completely re-made.

5 **usurped** captured (by the devil); stress on first syllable.

  **to another due** owing allegiance to another (i.e. God).

6 **to no end** to no avail.

7 Reason is God's deputy, planted in man to enable him to distinguish between right and wrong, and so should be available to 'defend' him from 'the crafts and assaults of the devil' (The Litany, *Book of Common Prayer*).

8 **captived** Stress second syllable.

9 **would be lovèd fain** very much wished to be loved.

10 **your enemy** the devil.

13 **enthral** enslave.

13–14 The paradoxes reinforce the idea of line 3. The lover image in
particular stresses the poet's sense of helplessness unless God will
take the initiative.

17

Since she whom I loved hath paid her last debt
To nature, and to hers, and my good is dead,
And her soul early into heaven ravishèd,
Wholly in heavenly things my mind is set.
Here the admiring her my mind did whet                               5
To seek thee God; so streams do show the head,
But though I have found thee, and thou my thirst hast fed,
A holy thirsty dropsy melts me yet.
But why should I beg more love, when as thou
Dost woo my soul for hers; offering all thine:                      10
And dost not only fear lest I allow
My love to saints and angels, things divine,
But in thy tender jealousy dost doubt
Lest the world, flesh, yea Devil put thee out.

1 **she whom I loved** Donne's wife died in 1617 at the age of thirty-
three.

1–2 **paid her last debt To nature** surrendered her life.

2 **to hers** a double ambiguity: 'she has paid her debts *to her family* and
my virtuous wife is dead'; or, 'she is dead *to her own good* and to
mine'. If the latter, then either: 'she cannot help herself or Donne (in
this world)'; or, 'her death is to the advantage of them both'.

5 **Here . . . whet** My love for her on earth made me eager . . .

6 **show the head** lead back to their source.

7 The image of the stream is related to Christ's words: 'the water that I
shall give him shall be in him a well of water springing up into
everlasting life' (John 4.14).

8 **dropsy**   an insatiable craving.

10 **for hers**   on her behalf.
   **offering all thine**   God offers all his love in dying on the cross to
   redeem man, enabling Donne to join his wife in heaven.

13 **tender jealousy**   God is seen as a lover.
   **doubt**   fear.

14 **world, flesh, yea Devil**   the three evils renounced in the Baptism
   Service; see lines 33–42 of 'Satire 3' (p58).
   **put thee out**   replace you in my affections.


# Hymn to God my God, in my Sickness

Since I am coming to that holy room,
    Where, with thy choir of saints for evermore,
I shall be made thy music; as I come
    I tune the instrument here at the door,
    And what I must do then, think here before.        5

Whilst my physicians by their love are grown
    Cosmographers, and I their map, who lie
Flat on this bed, that by them may be shown
    That this is my south-west discovery
    *Per fretum febris*, by these straits to die,     10

I joy, that in these straits, I see my west;
    For, though their currents yield return to none,
What shall my west hurt me? As west and east
    In all flat maps (and I am one) are one,
    So death doth touch the resurrectïon.     15

Is the Pacific Sea my home? Or are
    The eastern riches? Is Jerusalem?
Anyan, and Magellan, and Gibraltar,
    All straits, and none but straits, are ways to them,
    Whether where Japhet dwelt, or Cham, or Sem.    20

We think that Paradise and Calvary,
    Christ's Cross, and Adam's tree, stood in one place;
Look Lord, and find both Adams met in me;
    As the first Adam's sweat surrounds my face,
    May the last Adam's blood my soul embrace.        25

So, in his purple wrapped receive me Lord,
    By these his thorns give me his other crown;
And as to others' souls I preached thy word,
    Be this my text, my sermon to mine own,
    Therefore that he may raise the Lord throws down.    30

1  **that holy room**  heaven.

3  **thy music**  a musician in your service.

4  **I tune . . . door**  I prepare myself to make heavenly music by making the music of this poem before entering heaven.

6–7  The doctors bending over Donne in loving concern are like cosmographers (those who map the earth and the universe) bending over a map.

9  **south-west discovery**  a newly discovered sea route or the journey to death (south = heat and fever; west = sunset and death).

10  ***Per fretum febris***  through the heat or straits (a pun on *fretum*) of fever.
**straits**  narrow channel and terrible difficulties.

11  **west**  the New World and death.

14  **flat maps**  as opposed to the globe on which extreme west and east are seen to be the same place, just as death leads straight to resurrection and eternal life.

16–20  **Is the . . . Sem**  Every desirable place on earth (and heaven) can only be reached by travelling through straits (in both senses of the word). The whereabouts of Anyan is uncertain. The sons of Noah fathered the three main races after the flood: Japheth went to Europe, Ham to Africa, and Shem to Asia.

21–2  Adam's disobedience in eating the fruit of the forbidden tree alienated man from God and drove him from Paradise. The tradition that Christ's death on the tree (cross) on Calvary to reconcile man with God was in the same place emphasised God's providence for our salvation.

23  Christ was the second Adam: 'For as in Adam all die, even so in Christ shall all be made alive' (I Corinthians 15.22).

24  **sweat**  the punishment of Adam and all mankind: 'In the sweat of thy face shalt thou eat bread' (Genesis 3.19).

25  Christ's blood washes and redeems his soul.

26  **purple**  Christ's blood; the imperial robe of Christ the king; Donne's feverish high colour.

27  **his thorns**  Christ's crown of thorns on the cross and Donne's own sufferings.
    **other crown**  his reward in heaven.

29  The last line of the poem is the 'text' on which he bases a sermon addressed to himself.

30  **Therefore . . . down**  God sends death in order that he may raise man to eternal life.

# A Hymn to God the Father

Wilt thou forgive that sin where I begun,
   Which was my sin, though it were done before?
Wilt thou forgive that sin, through which I run,
   And do run still: though still I do deplore?
     When thou hast done, thou hast not done,        5
       For, I have more.

Wilt thou forgive that sin which I have won
   Others to sin? and, made my sin their door?
Wilt thou forgive that sin which I did shun
   A year, or two: but wallowed in, a score?        10
     When thou hast done, thou hast not done,
       For I have more.

I have a sin of fear, that when I have spun
   My last thread, I shall perish on the shore;
But swear by thy self, that at my death thy son        15
   Shall shine as he shines now, and heretofore;
     And, having done that, thou hast done,
       I fear no more.

1 **that sin where I begun**  original sin, the inborn tendency to sin inherited by all mankind from Adam who sinned 'before'.

3 **through which I run**  which I am in the habit of committing.

4 **still**  always.

5 **done**  finished (forgiving my sins); also a pun on his own name, John Donne.

6 **more**  more sins.

8 **their door**  The example of Donne's sins has been a 'door' through which others have passed to sin.

10 **wallowed in**  enjoyed without restraint.

13 **a sin of fear**  to despair of God's power to save was the ultimate sin because it cut man off from God.

13–14 **spun My last thread**  lived my last moment.

14 **shore**  the gap between life and death, between this world and the next.

15 **son**  God's son is also the Sun of Righteousness whose light will disperse the shadows of sin and death.

17 **thou hast done**  you have finished forgiving me and therefore you possess me, John Donne.

# George Herbert
## 1593–1633

## Affliction (1)

When first thou didst entice to thee my heart,
      I thought the service brave:
So many joys I writ down for my part,
      Besides what I might have
Out of my stock of natural delights,            5
Augmented with thy gracious benefits.

I lookèd on thy furniture so fine,
      And made it fine to me:
Thy glorious household-stuff did me entwine,
      And 'tice me unto thee.          10
Such stars I counted mine: both heaven and earth
Paid me my wages in a world of mirth.

What pleasures could I want, whose King I served?
      Where joys my fellows were.
Thus argued into hopes, my thoughts reserved      15
      No place for grief or fear.
Therefore my sudden soul caught at the place,
And made her youth and fierceness seek thy face.

At first thou gav'st me milk and sweetnesses;
      I had my wish and way:        20
My days were strawed with flowers and happiness;
      There was no month but May.
But with my years sorrow did twist and grow,
And made a party unawares for woe.

My flesh began unto my soul in pain,       25
      Sicknesses cleave my bones;

Consuming agues dwell in every vein,
     And tune my breath to groans.
Sorrow was all my soul; I scarce believed,
    Till grief did tell me roundly, that I lived.        30

When I got health, thou took'st away my life,
     And more; for my friends die:
My mirth and edge was lost; a blunted knife
     Was of more use than I.
Thus thin and lean without a fence or friend,        35
I was blown through with every storm and wind.

Whereas my birth and spirit rather took
     The way that takes the town;
Thou didst betray me to a lingering book,
     And wrap me in a gown.        40
I was entangled in the world of strife,
Before I had the power to change my life.

Yet, for I threatened oft the siege to raise,
     Not simpering all mine age,
Thou often didst with Academic praise        45
     Melt and dissolve my rage.
I took thy sweetened pill, till I came where
I could not go away, nor persevere.

Yet lest perchance I should too happy be
     In my unhappiness,        50
Turning my purge to food, thou throwest me
     Into more sicknesses.
Thus doth thy power cross-bias me, not making
Thine own gift good, yet me from my ways taking.

Now I am here, what thou wilt do with me        55
     None of my books will show:
I read, and sigh, and wish I were a tree;
     For sure then I should grow
To fruit or shade: at least some bird would trust
Her household to me, and I should be just.        60

Yet, though thou troublest me, I must be meek;
    In weakness must be stout.
Well, I will change the service, and go seek
    Some other master out.
Ah my dear God! though I am clean forgot,        65
Let me not love thee, if I love thee not.

**Affliction** spiritual suffering. (A number of Herbert's poems have the same titles; hence the numbers in brackets.)

2 **brave** splendid; perhaps the fine livery of the servant.

3 **I writ down for my part** I expected to have.

6 **gracious benefits** God's grace is freely given.

7–9 Just as the servant of an earthly master might be impressed by splendid household furnishings so Herbert is attracted by all that is associated with religion, including quite literally church furnishings.

10 **'tice** entice.

11 **stars** heavenly treasures.

13 **want** lack.
    **whose King** God is the King of 'pleasures'. There is doubtless a reference here to Herbert's ambitious service of James I which failed to lead to the promotion that he had hoped for.

15–16 **Thus argued . . . fear** My happiness made me optimistic without any thought of grief or fear.

17–18 **Therefore . . . face** My impetuous soul eagerly took up the appointment (but was also trapped) and turned her fierce, youthful energy to seeking your (God's) face.

19 **milk and sweetnesses** images of heavenly bliss.

21 **strawed with flowers** covered with scattered flowers.

23 **with my years** with advancing age.

24 **party** conspiracy.

25 **began** began to speak; the next three lines are spoken by the body to the soul.

27 **agues** fevers.

30 **roundly** plainly.

33 **edge** eagerness.

37–8 **Whereas . . . town** Although my breeding and character inclined me to court and city life . . .

39 **lingering** This suggests the tameness of a life devoted to academic study.

40 **gown** worn by the university don and the priest.

43 **the siege** the means by which God prevents him from following a worldly life.

44 **simpering** smiling in a silly or insincere way.

51 **purge** purgative.

53–4 In a game of bowls the bias makes each bowl change its direction. God's power has turned him away from his own 'ways', but has not led to spiritual fulfilment either.

60 As a man he is not 'just' (justified in the sight of God), but as a tree he would be 'just' (the tree adequately fulfilling its proper functions).

61 **meek** piously submissive to injury.

62 **stout** brave.

65 **though I am clean forgot** although I have quite forgotten myself (in complaining like this), or, although I am quite forgotten.

66 This appears to be a plea that he should be released from his tormenting love for God, but the ruefully affectionate tone of 'Ah my dear God', a possible pun on 'let' (meaning perhaps 'hinder' as well as 'allow') and the doubt implied by 'if' all combine to suggest a continuing love of God.

# The Agony

    Philosophers have measured mountains,
Fathomed the depths of seas, of states, and kings,
Walked with a staff to heaven, and tracèd fountains:
    But there are two vast, spacious things,
The which to measure it doth more behove:       5
Yet few there are that sound them; Sin and Love.

    Who would know Sin, let him repair
Unto Mount Olivet; there shall he see
A man so wrung with pains, that all his hair,
    His skin, his garments bloody be.      10
Sin is that press and vice, which forceth pain
To hunt his cruel food through every vein.

Who knows not Love, let him assay
And taste that juice, which on the cross a pike
Did set again abroach; then let him say                    15
  If ever he did taste the like.
Love is that liquor sweet and most divine,
Which my God feels as blood; but I, as wine.

1  **philosophers** a wide term including scientists.

3  **staff** measuring rod.
   **fountains** sources of rivers.

5  **it doth more behove** it is more morally fitting.

6  **sound** measure to its depth.

8  **Mount Olivet** the site of the Garden of Gethsemane where Jesus
   prayed in agony on the night of his arrest before his crucifixion the
   next day.

9–10 'And being in an agony he prayed more earnestly: and his sweat was
   as it were great drops of blood falling down to the ground' (Luke
   22.44).

11  **press** Sin causes Christ's agony in the Garden and his death on the
   cross; it is the wine-press that forces from Christ (traditionally shown
   as a cluster of grapes, see introduction, p18) his sweat and the blood
   that is commemorated in the wine of the Holy Communion or Mass.

13  **assay** test the quality.

14  'But one of the soldiers with a spear pierced his side, and forthwith
   came there out blood and water' (John 19.34).

15  **set . . . abroach** to pierce a barrel and leave running.

17–18 Christ's death on the cross is the supreme demonstration of love and
   the blood that he shed is the sweet, life-giving wine of the Holy
   Communion.

# Bitter-Sweet

Ah my dear angry Lord,
Since thou dost love, yet strike;
Cast down, yet help afford;
Sure I will do the like.

I will complain, yet praise;                                          5
I will bewail, approve:
And all my sour-sweet days
I will lament, and love.


# The Collar

I struck the board, and cried, No more.
            I will abroad.
What? shall I ever sigh and pine?
My lines and life are free; free as the road,
    Loose as the wind, as large as store.          5
            Shall I be still in suit?
    Have I no harvest but a thorn
    To let me blood, and not restore
    What I have lost with cordial fruit?
            Sure there was wine          10
Before my sighs did dry it: there was corn
            Before my tears did drown it.
    Is the year only lost to me?
            Have I no bays to crown it?
No flowers, no garlands gay? all blasted?          15
            All wasted?
    Not so, my heart: but there is fruit,
            And thou hast hands.
    Recover all thy sigh-blown age
On double pleasures: leave thy cold dispute          20
Of what is fit, and not. Forsake thy cage,
            Thy rope of sands,
Which petty thoughts have made, and made to thee
    Good cable, to enforce and draw,
            And be thy law,          25
    While thou didst wink and wouldst not see.
            Away; take heed:
            I will abroad.
Call in thy death's head there: tie up thy fears.

He that forbears                                    30
To suit and serve his need,
Deserves his load.
But as I raved and grew more fierce and wild
At every word,
Me thoughts I heard one calling, *Child*:            35
And I replied, *My Lord*.

This poem may be read as the protest of a priest who wishes to escape the constraining 'collar' of devotion to God and who expresses his choler (anger). Ironically, however, he expresses his suffering in terms similar to those of Christ ('a thorn To let me blood') whose love for him and all mankind has been shown on the cross long before. His response to God's affectionate voice at the end of the poem, therefore, is striking but nonetheless understandable.

1 **board** table; the altar on which the Holy Communion was celebrated.

2 **abroad** away.

4 **My lines** my lot in life.

6 **still in suit** always begging.

9 **cordial** restorative (especially of medicines for the heart).

10-12 The bread and wine of the Holy Communion no longer comfort him.

14 **bays** a wreath of bay leaves for a conqueror or successful poet (very different from Christ's crown of thorns).

17-18 He can rebel like Adam and Eve.

21 **fit** morally right.

22-5 He deludes himself in thinking that the restrictions that bind him to God are 'Good cable'; they are as ineffective as a 'rope of sands'.

26 **While . . . see** while you shut your eyes and did not wish to look.

29 **death's head** a skull used as a reminder of death's inevitability (and therefore of the need to repent).

30-2 **He that . . . load** He who refrains from looking after his own interests deserves to suffer.

# Denial

When my devotions could not pierce
Thy silent ears;
Then was my heart broken, as was my verse:
My breast was full of fears
And disorder:                                    5

My bent thoughts, like a brittle bow,
Did fly asunder:
Each took his way; some would to pleasures go,
Some to the wars and thunder
Of alarms.                                      10

As good go anywhere, they say,
As to benumb
Both knees and heart, in crying night and day,
*Come, come, my God, O come,*
But no hearing.                                 15

O that thou shouldst give dust a tongue
To cry to thee,
And then not hear it crying! all day long
My heart was in my knee,
But no hearing.                                 20

Therefore my soul lay out of sight,
Untuned, unstrung:
My feeble spirit, unable to look right,
Like a nipped blossom, hung
Discontented.                                   25

O cheer and tune my heartless breast,
Defer no time;
That so thy favours granting my request,
They and my mind may chime,
And mend my rhyme.                              30

3 **verse** an ordered poetic structure (and so an image of order and of harmony between God and man).

5 **disorder** spiritual confusion, but also 'unrhymed', as are all the last
   lines until the final stanza.

6 **bent** a paradoxical pun: directed a certain way, or bending away
   from it. The disobedient Jews are described as 'starting aside like a
   broken bow' (Psalm 78.58).

16 **dust** man: 'for dust thou art, and unto dust shalt thou return'
   (Genesis 3.19).

22 **unstrung** i.e. like an unused musical instrument.

23 **right** straight ahead.

26 **heartless** disheartened.


# Easter

Rise heart; thy Lord is risen. Sing his praise
               Without delays,
Who takes thee by the hand, that thou likewise
               With him mayst rise:
That, as his death calcinèd thee to dust,          5
His life may make thee gold, and much more just.

Awake, my lute, and struggle for thy part
               With all thy art.
The cross taught all wood to resound his name,
               Who bore the same.      10
His stretchèd sinews taught all strings, what key
Is best to celebrate this most high day.

Consort both heart and lute, and twist a song
               Pleasant and long:
Or since all music is but three parts vied       15
               And multiplied;
O let thy blessèd Spirit bear a part,
And make up our defects with his sweet art.

I got me flowers to straw thy way;
I got me boughs off many a tree:          20
But thou wast up by break of day,
And broughtst thy sweets along with thee.

The Sun arising in the East,
Though he give light and the East perfume;
If they should offer to contest                                    25
With thy arising, they presume.

Can there be any day but this,
Though many suns to shine endeavour?
We count three hundred, but we miss:
There is but one, and that one ever.                               30

   1  Compare the words of the *Sursum Corda* in the Holy Communion:
     'Lift up your hearts.' 'We lift them up unto the Lord.'

   5  **calcinèd**  burned to ashes, but also refined by fire (an alchemical
     expression).

   6  Alchemists believed that the philosopher's stone would turn base
     metal into gold; similarly Christ's life transforms Christians.

  10  **Who . . . same**  which carried Christ.

11–12  Christ's body stretched on the cross is compared to the strings
     stretched on a wooden lute.

  13  **Consort**  perform music together; stress second syllable.
     **twist**  interweave the lines of music.

  15  **parts**  the lines of music which together will complete the harmony if
     the Holy Spirit joins in.
     **vied**  increased by repetition as in the imitation of counterpoint:
     where each voice enters in turn with the same musical phrase.

  17  **bear**  perform.

  19  **straw thy way**  scatter in thy path. Compare the story of Palm
     Sunday.

19–30  The change in verse form marks the 'song' referred to in line 13.

  24  Perfumes were imported from the East.

29–30  **We count . . . ever**  We count a sunrise on every day of the year, but
     we are mistaken. The Son of God rose only once from the dead and
     he will never set again.

# Easter Wings

Lord, who createdst man in wealth and store,
Though foolishly he lost the same,
Decaying more and more,
Til he became
Most poor: 5
With thee
O let me rise
As larks, harmoniously,
And sing this day thy victories:
Then shall the fall further the flight in me. 10

My tender age in sorrow did begin:
And still with sicknesses and shame
Thou didst so punish sin,
That I became
Most thin. 15
With thee
Let me combine,
And feel this day thy victory:
For, if I imp my wing on thine,
Affliction shall advance the flight in me. 20

Both the title and the pattern recall a passage in Malachi which is also suggested by the son/sun pun of 'Easter' (printed immediately before this in the original): 'But unto you that fear my name shall the Sun of righteousness arise with healing in his wings' (Malachi 4.2).

1–2 In Paradise man had all that he needed ('wealth and store') until he 'lost' it by disobeying God.

10 Paradoxically the 'fall' (the disobedience of Adam and Eve in Paradise) now leads to Herbert's rising in flight. Compare line 20.

19 **imp** to graft feathers on to a bird's wing.

# The Elixir

Teach me, my God and King,
In all things thee to see,
And what I do in any thing,
To do it as for thee:

Not rudely, as a beast,                                          5
  To run into an action;
But still to make thee prepossessed,
  And give it his perfection.

A man that looks on glass,
  On it may stay his eye;                                        10
Or if he pleaseth, through it pass,
  And then the heaven espy.

All may of thee partake:
  Nothing can be so mean,
Which with his tincture (for thy sake)                           15
  Will not grow bright and clean.

A servant with this clause
  Makes drudgery divine:
Who sweeps a room, as for thy laws,
  Makes that and the action fine.                                20

This is the famous stone
  That turneth all to gold:
For that which God doth touch and own
  Cannot for less be told.

**The Elixir**  a preparation supposed to turn base metals into gold,
often associated with the philosopher's stone (see lines 21–2 and
'Easter', line 6).

5  **rudely**  without thought.

7–8  **But still . . . perfection**  But to dedicate every action to 'thee' (God) in
advance and do it perfectly.

9–12  A man's view of life may be limited or he may perceive the heavenly
implications of every act.

15  In alchemy a 'tincture' is an abstract principle that can be instilled
into a material substance. Here the tincture of dedication to God
('for thy sake') is being instilled into even the humblest of actions.

23  **touch**  to test the purity of gold by rubbing it on a touchstone.

24  **told**  valued.

# The Flower

How fresh, O Lord, how sweet and clean
Are thy returns! Ev'n as the flowers in spring;
    To which, besides their own demean,
The late-past frosts tributes of pleasure bring.
               Grief melts away          5
               Like snow in May,
    As if there were no such cold thing.

Who would have thought my shrivelled heart
Could have recovered greenness? It was gone
    Quite under ground; as flowers depart       10
To see their mother-root, when they have blown;
               Where they together
               All the hard weather,
    Dead to the world, keep house unknown.

These are thy wonders, Lord of power,       15
Killing and quickening, bringing down to hell
    And up to heaven in an hour;
Making a chiming of a passing-bell.
               We say amiss,
               This or that is:       20
    Thy word is all, if we could spell.

O that I once past changing were,
Fast in thy Paradise, where no flower can wither!
    Many a spring I shoot up fair,
Offering at heaven, growing and groaning thither:     25
               Nor doth my flower
               Want a spring-shower,
    My sins and I joining together:

But while I grow in a straight line,
Still upwards bent, as if heaven were mine own,     30
    Thy anger comes, and I decline:

What frost to that? what pole is not the zone,
>     Where all things burn,
>     When thou dost turn,
And the least frown of thine is shown?                          35

And now in age I bud again,
After so many deaths I live and write;
I once more smell the dew and rain,
And relish versing: O my only light,
>     It cannot be                                             40
>     That I am he
On whom thy tempests fell all night.

These are thy wonders, Lord of love,
To make us see we are but flowers that glide:
Which when we once can find and prove,                          45
Thou hast a garden for us, where to bide.
>     Who would be more,
>     Swelling through store,
Forfeit their Paradise by their pride.

3 **demean** bearing or appearance.

11 **blown** blossomed.

18 **chiming** not just a sweet noise, but one that is 'in tune' with God; compare end of 'Denial' (p82).

21 **spell** read or decipher God's 'word' in all that happens.

25 **Offering** aiming.

27 **Want** lack.

30 **bent** directed.

32 **zone** the torrid or tropical zone.

44 **glide** quietly pass away.

45 **prove** experience (death).

48 swollen roots provide food for the winter (e.g. daffodil bulbs), but here 'swelling with pride in their worldly goods'.

# Hope

I gave to Hope a watch of mine: but he
        An anchor gave to me.
Then an old prayer-book I did present:
        And he an optic sent.
With that I gave a vial full of tears:            5
        But he a few green ears:
Ah Loiterer! I'll no more, no more I'll bring:
        I did expect a ring.

The poet's gifts to Hope symbolise his long wait, his many prayers
and his sufferings. In return he is given an anchor (the symbol of
hope) to hold fast by, an 'optic' or telescope so that he can 'the
heaven espy' and an incomplete and unripe harvest. He is
disappointed because he had hoped for 'a ring', the symbol of
marriage or unity with God.

5–6 Compare with 'The Collar', lines 11–12 (p80).

# Jordan (2)

When first my lines of heavenly joys made mention,
Such was their lustre, they did so excel,
That I sought out quaint words, and trim invention;
My thoughts began to burnish, sprout, and swell,
Curling with metaphors a plain intention,      5
Decking the sense, as if it were to sell.

Thousands of notions in my brain did run,
Offering their service, if I were not sped:
I often blotted what I had begun;
This was not quick enough, and that was dead.     10
Nothing could seem too rich to clothe the sun,
Much less those joys which trample on his head.

As flames do work and wind, when they ascend,
So did I weave myself into the sense.

But while I bustled, I might hear a friend                              15
Whisper, *How wide is all this long pretence!*
*There is in love a sweetness ready penned:*
*Copy out only that, and save expense.*

**Jordan** The river which the Jews crossed to reach the Promised Land and the river in which Jesus was baptised. It therefore symbolises the making of a fresh start (conversion) and the washing away of sins. This in turn implies a new approach to writing poetry.

1   **lines** of poetry.

3   **quaint** ingeniously elegant.
   **invention** a rhetorical term meaning here devising a literary way of treating the subject.

6   **Decking ... sell** dressing up the sense as if it were an object to be sold.

8   **not sped** unsuccessful.

9   **blotted** obliterated.

10   **quick** lively as opposed to 'dead'.

11   **sun** sun/Son of God.

14   Compare with Marvell's 'The Coronet', lines 13–16 (p119) for the concept of ulterior and selfish motives being woven or intertwined with a work of art supposedly dedicated to God alone.

# Justice (1)

I cannot skill of these thy ways.
*Lord, thou didst make me, yet thou woundest me;*
*Lord, thou dost wound me, yet thou dost relieve me:*
*Lord, thou relievest, yet I die by thee:*
*Lord, thou dost kill me, yet thou dost reprieve me.*        5

But when I mark my life and praise,
    Thy justice me most fitly pays:
For, *I do praise thee, yet I praise thee not:*
*My prayers mean thee, yet my prayers stray:*
*I would do well, yet sin the hand hath got:*               10
*My soul doth love thee, yet it loves delay.*
    I cannot skill of these my ways.

Herbert is puzzled by the apparent inconsistency of God's treatment
of him until he recognises how it matches the inconsistency of his
own ways.

1 **skill of** understand.

10 **hand** upper hand.

# Life

I made a posy, while the day ran by:
Here will I smell my remnants out, and tie
    My life within this band.
But time did beckon to the flowers, and they
By noon most cunningly did steal away,        5
    And withered in my hand.

My hand was next to them, and then my heart:
I took, without more thinking, in good part
    Time's gentle admonition:
Who did so sweetly death's sad taste convey,      10
Making my mind to smell my fatal day;
    Yet sugaring the suspicion.

Farewell dear flowers, sweetly your time ye spent,
Fit, while ye lived, for smell or ornament,
    And after death for cures.      15
I follow straight without complaints or grief,
Since if my scent be good, I care not, if
    It be as short as yours.

1 **posy** a bunch of flowers, but also a motto.

7 **and then my heart** He took to heart the lesson to be learned from the
death of the flowers.

15 **cures** i.e. as medicinal herbs.

16 **follow** i.e. to death.

# Love (3)

Love bade me welcome: yet my soul drew back,
     Guilty of dust and sin.
But quick-eyed Love, observing me grow slack
     From my first entrance in,
Drew nearer to me, sweetly questioning,         5
     If I lacked any thing.

A guest, I answered, worthy to be here:
     Love said, You shall be he.
I the unkind, ungrateful? Ah my dear,
     I cannot look on thee.         10
Love took my hand, and smiling did reply,
     Who made the eyes but I?

Truth Lord, but I have marred them: let my shame
     Go where it doth deserve.
And know you not, says Love, who bore the blame?    15
     My dear, then I will serve.
You must sit down, says Love, and taste my meat:
     So I did sit and eat.

**Love** 'God is love' (1 John 4.16). This is the last poem in the main section of his poetry as Herbert organised it. It deals with the soul's acceptance into communion with God in Heaven rather than simply in the Holy Communion service, for it is based on a passage in which Jesus condemns concern for things of this life, since death may come at any time and then 'Blessed are those servants, whom the lord when he cometh shall find watching . . . he shall gird himself, and make them to sit down to meat, and will come forth and serve them' (Luke 12.37).

2  **dust and sin** the consequences of the journey of life.

15  Christ 'Who his own self bare our sins in his own body on the tree, that we, being dead to sins, should live unto righteousness' (1 Peter 2.24).

16  **serve** at table.

17  **my meat** Christ's body and eternal life; as the priest gives the bread in the Holy Communion he says: 'The Body of our Lord Jesus Christ, which was given for thee, preserve thy body and soul unto everlasting life.'

# Mary Magdalene

When blessèd Mary wiped her Saviour's feet,
(Whose precepts she had trampled on before)
And wore them for a jewel on her head,
    Showing his steps should be the street,
    Wherein she thenceforth evermore          5
With pensive humbleness would live and tread:

She being stained her self, why did she strive
To make him clean, who could not be defiled?
Why kept she not her tears for her own faults,
    And not his feet? Though we could dive       10
    In tears like seas, our sins are piled
Deeper than they, in words, and works, and thoughts.

Dear soul, she knew who did vouchsafe and deign
To bear her filth; and that her sins did dash
Ev'n God himself: wherefore she was not loth,      15
    As she had brought wherewith to stain,
    So to bring in wherewith to wash:
And yet in washing one, she washèd both.

**Mary Magdalene** St Luke tells the story of a woman who 'was a
sinner' (traditionally thought to be Mary Magdalene) who washed
Christ's feet with her tears, wiped them with her hair and then
anointed them with ointment. Her sins were forgiven because 'she
loved much' (Luke 7.36–50).

2  **precepts** moral commands.

4–6  She is going to follow the example of his life. The image of a 'street'
to follow is suggested by Christ's saying: 'I am the way . . . no man
cometh unto the Father, but by me' (John 14.6).

7  **stained** with sin.

8  Jesus is sinless.

10–12  **Though . . . thoughts** Even if our tears of repentance were as deep as
seas our sins of every kind would still be even greater. (The general
confession in the Holy Communion speaks of sins 'committed by
thought, word, and deed'.)

13  **who did vouchsafe and deign** who willingly agreed to humble
himself (i.e. Christ).

14 **filth** sin.
   **dash** bespatter with dirt.
15 **loth** reluctant.
16 **wherewith to stain** i.e. her sins.
17 **wherewith to wash** i.e. her tears.
18 **both** She not only washed Christ's feet, but also helped to wash
   away her own sins.


# The Pulley

When God at first made man,
Having a glass of blessings standing by;
Let us (said he) pour on him all we can:
Let the world's riches, which dispersèd lie,
    Contract into a span.                                5

So strength first made a way;
Then beauty flowed, then wisdom, honour, pleasure:
When almost all was out, God made a stay,
Perceiving that alone of all his treasure
    Rest in the bottom lay.                            10

For if I should (said he)
Bestow this jewel also on my creature,
He would adore my gifts instead of me,
And rest in Nature, not the God of Nature:
    So both should losers be.                          15

Yet let him keep the rest,
But keep them with repining restlessness:
Let him be rich and weary, that at least,
If goodness lead him not, yet weariness
    May toss him to my breast.                         20

The 'pulley' is man's need for rest which will draw him back to God.
The pun on rest (tranquillity/remainder) embodies the theme of the
poem.

5 **span** a small space.

8 **made a stay**  paused.

12 **my creature**  man (created by God).

14 **And rest . . . Nature**  find comfort in/depend on Nature and not on Nature's Creator.

15 **both**  God and man.

20 **breast**  the place of rest, the very sound of which is included in this final rhyme word.

# Redemption

Having been tenant long to a rich Lord,
   Not thriving, I resolvèd to be bold,
   And make a suit unto him, to afford
A new small-rented lease, and cancel the old.

In heaven at his manor I him sought:              5
   They told me there, that he was lately gone
   About some land, which he had dearly bought
Long since on earth, to take possessïon.

I straight returned, and knowing his great birth,
   Sought him accordingly in great resorts;         10
   In cities, theatres, gardens, parks, and courts:
At length I heard a ragged noise and mirth

   Of thieves and murderers: there I him espied,
   Who straight, *Your suit is granted*, said, and died.

In Christian teaching the old agreement (or testament) between God and man was replaced by a new agreement when Christ demonstrated his love by paying the price of sin (suffering the death penalty on the cross) on man's behalf. Christ makes this clear just before his death when at the Last Supper he gives the disciples wine saying: 'Drink ye all of this; for this is my blood of the New Testament, which is shed for you and for many for the remission [forgiveness] of sins.' (See both the prayer of consecration in the Holy Communion and the story in Matthew 26, especially verses 26–9.) Here the new agreement or testament is represented by the new lease that the poet requests.

3  **suit**  request.

13  'Behold a man gluttonous, and a winebibber, a friend of publicans
and sinners' (Matthew 11.19); 'And with him they crucify two
thieves' (Mark 15.27).

14  Christ's death is necessary for the granting of the suit. (The original
title was 'The Passion'.)

# Time

Meeting with Time, slack thing, said I,
Thy scythe is dull; whet it for shame.
No marvel Sir, he did reply,
If it at length deserve some blame:
    But where one man would have me grind it,      5
    Twenty for one too sharp do find it.

Perhaps some such of old did pass,
Who above all things loved this life;
To whom thy scythe a hatchet was,
Which now is but a pruning-knife.      10
    Christ's coming hath made man thy debtor,
    Since by thy cutting he grows better.

And in his blessing thou art blest:
For where thou only wert before
An executioner at best;      15
Thou art a gardener now, and more,
    An usher to convey our souls
    Beyond the utmost stars and poles.

And this is that makes life so long,
While it detains us from our God.      20
Ev'n pleasures here increase the wrong,
And length of days lengthen the rod.
    Who wants the place, where God doth dwell,
    Partakes already half of hell.

Of what strange length must that needs be,                          25
Which ev'n eternity excludes!
Thus far Time heard me patiently:
Then chafing said, This man deludes:
 What do I here before his door?
 He doth not crave less time, but more.                        30

**Time** traditionally portrayed as a figure with an hourglass and a scythe, since time brings death: 'All flesh is grass . . . The grass withereth' (Isaiah 40.6–7).

 2 **whet** sharpen.

9–10 The 'hatchet' kills, but the gardener's 'pruning-knife' makes possible new growth and life.

 11 Man is indebted to Death since it opens the way to eternal life thanks to Christ's redemptive action.

 17 **usher** one who leads guests into the royal (divine) presence.

 18 **Beyond . . . poles** beyond the limits of the universe.

 19 **this is** it is this.

 22 **rod** punishment.

 23 **wants the place** is absent from.

25–6 **Of what . . . excludes!** How strangely long must that thing (life on earth) necessarily be that prevents man from enjoying eternal life!

 28 **chafing** becoming impatient.
   **deludes** is mistaken/is tricking me.

 30 **crave** beg for.
   **more** i.e. eternal life.

# Vanity (1)

   The fleet Astronomer can bore,
And thread the spheres with his quick-piercing mind:
He views their stations, walks from door to door,
   Surveys, as if he had designed
To make a purchase there: he sees their dances,              5

And knoweth long before,
Both their full-eyed aspects, and secret glances.

The nimble Diver with his side
Cuts through the working waves, that he may fetch
His dearly-earnèd pearl, which God did hide                    10
On purpose from the venturous wretch;
That he might save his life, and also hers,
Who with excessive pride
Her own destruction and his danger wears.

The subtle Chymick can divest                                 15
And strip the creature naked, till he find
The callow principles within their nest:
There he imparts to them his mind,
Admitted to their bed-chamber, before
They appear trim and dressed                                  20
To ordinary suitors at the door.

What hath not man sought out and found,
But his dear God? who yet his glorious law
Embosoms in us, mellowing the ground
With showers and frosts, with love and awe,                   25
So that we need not say, Where's this command?
Poor man, thou searchest round
To find out *death*, but missest *life* at hand.

**Vanity** the empty folly of man's activities as described in the first
three stanzas: 'Vanity of vanities, saith the preacher; all is vanity'
(Ecclesiastes 12.8).

1–2 'Fleet', 'bore' and 'quick-piercing' all suggest the speed and
     penetration of the Astronomer's understanding of the hollow,
     concentric, crystal spheres whose movements caused (supposedly) the
     movements of the heavenly bodies.

3–5 He surveys the heavens as easily as a prospective purchaser surveys a
     house ('designed' = planned).

 5 **dances** patterned movements.

 7 **aspects** positions as seen from earth; stress second syllable.

 9 **working** rising and falling.

11 **venturous** daring.

14 **destruction** The woman's pride in her jewelry will lead to her moral downfall.

15 **Chymick** chemist.
**divest** remove the covering.

17 **callow** unfledged, without feathers (and therefore basic).

18–21 A favoured suitor might be admitted to a great man's chamber before he was fully dressed.

23 **But** except.

24 **Embosoms in us** puts in our hearts.

24–5 We are like ground prepared for the seed of God's law by showers of love and the frost of awe (fearful respect).

28 **at hand** close at hand.


# Virtue

Sweet day, so cool, so calm, so bright,
The bridal of the earth and sky:
The dew shall weep thy fall tonight;
   For thou must die.

Sweet rose, whose hue angry and brave    5
Bids the rash gazer wipe his eye:
Thy root is ever in its grave,
   And thou must die.

Sweet spring, full of sweet days and roses,
A box where sweets compacted lie;    10
My music shows ye have your closes,
   And all must die.

Only a sweet and virtuous soul,
Like seasoned timber, never gives;
But though the whole world turn to coal,    15
   Then chiefly lives.

2 **bridal** wedding.

3 **fall** not only night, but also sin and death.

5 **angry and brave** red (the colour of anger) and making a fine show.

10 **sweets** perfumes.

11 **music** pattern of verse with its refrain.
**closes** ends; also cadences at the end of musical phrases.

14 **gives** gives way.

15–16 **coal** When all is consumed with fire at the end of the world (like 'coal') the 'virtuous soul' will live on in heaven.


# The Windows

Lord, how can man preach thy eternal word?
        He is a brittle crazy glass:
Yet in thy temple thou dost him afford
        This glorious and transcendent place,
        To be a window, through thy grace.     5

But when thou dost anneal in glass thy story,
        Making thy life to shine within
The holy preacher's; then the light and glory
        More reverend grows, and more doth win:
        Which else shows waterish, bleak, and thin.   10

Doctrine and life, colours and light, in one
        When they combine and mingle, bring
A strong regard and awe: but speech alone
        Doth vanish like a flaring thing,
        And in the ear, not conscience ring.   15

2 **crazy** cracked.

3 **afford** give.

4 **transcendent** pre-eminent.

5 **grace** God's favour (unmerited, but strengthening).

6 **anneal** burn colours into glass; stained-glass windows present biblical stories.

9 **win** When God's life shines within the life of a preacher like light shining through a stained-glass window, the listeners are 'won' over by the preaching that would otherwise ('else') be unconvincing.

11 **Doctrine** teaching of the Church.

13 **alone** by itself; the priest whose preaching is not illumined by the practice of what he preaches will never touch the consciences of his congregation.

# A Wreath

A wreathèd garland of deservèd praise,
Of praise deservèd, unto thee I give,
I give to thee, who knowest all my ways,
My crooked winding ways, wherein I live,
Wherein I die, not live: for life is straight,          5
Straight as a line, and ever tends to thee,
To thee, who art more far above deceit,
Than deceit seems above simplicity.
Give me simplicity, that I may live,
So live and like, that I may know thy ways,          10
Know them and practise them: then shall I give
For this poor wreath, give thee a crown of praise.

6 **tends to** leads towards.

12 **a crown of praise** The wreath is completed in the echoing of the first line of the poem.

# Andrew Marvell
## 1621–1678

## To His Coy Mistress

Had we but world enough, and time,
This coyness, Lady, were no crime.
We would sit down, and think which way
To walk, and pass our long love's day.
Thou by the Indian Ganges' side                          5
Shouldst rubies find: I by the tide
Of Humber would complain. I would
Love you ten years before the flood:
And you should, if you please, refuse
Till the conversion of the Jews.                         10
My vegetable love should grow
Vaster than empires, and more slow.
An hundred years should go to praise
Thine eyes, and on thy forehead gaze.
Two hundred to adore each breast:                        15
But thirty thousand to the rest.
An age at least to every part,
And the last age should show your heart:
For, Lady, you deserve this state;
Nor would I love at lower rate.                          20
    But at my back I always hear
Time's wingèd chariot hurrying near:
And yonder all before us lie
Deserts of vast eternity.
Thy beauty shall no more be found;                       25
Nor, in thy marble vault, shall sound
My echoing song: then worms shall try
That long-preserved virginity:

And your quaint honour turn to dust;
And into ashes all my lust.                               30
The grave's a fine and private place,
But none, I think, do there embrace.
     Now, therefore, while the youthful hue
Sits on thy skin like morning dew,
And while thy willing soul transpires                     35
At every pore with instant fires,
Now let us sport us while we may;
And now, like amorous birds of prey,
Rather at once our time devour,
Than languish in his slow-chapped power.                  40
Let us roll all our strength, and all
Our sweetness, up into one ball:
And tear our pleasures with rough strife,
Thorough the iron gates of life.
Thus, though we cannot make our sun                       45
Stand still, yet we will make him run.

This invitation to love is argued in the form of a syllogism (two premises: 'Had we but world enough, and time', 'But . . .' and a conclusion: 'Now, therefore . . .'). 'Coy' means modest, without its modern overtones of hypocrisy, and 'Mistress' simply means the woman that the poet loves, again without the modern meaning.

1 **but** only.

7 **Humber** While she visited the exotic east he would stay at home (Hull) to write his lover's laments ('complain').

8–10 He will love from almost the beginning of history (before Noah's flood) until its end ('the conversion of the Jews' is unlikely to be much sooner!).

11 **vegetable** capable of growth, but lacking the senses and reason.

19 **state** ceremonious treatment.

20 **rate** cost.

26 **marble vault** i.e. burying place.

29 **quaint honour** fastidious chastity; the last quotation given in the *Oxford English Dictionary* for 'quaint' in its Chaucerian sense of pudenda is dated 1598, but possibly a pun is intended; 'honour' had a similar meaning.

33  **hue** complexion. In her edition of Vaughan's poems E. S. Donno
follows the reading 'glue' i.e. life which glues body and soul
together. This reading might also suggest sweating passion when
taken in conjunction with 'dew' and 'instant fires'; compare Donne's
poem 'The Ecstasy', lines 5–6 (p34).

35  **transpires** passes through the skin.

37  **sport us** enjoy ourselves.

38  **birds of prey** The birds of prey feeding on flesh are an image of
lovers with strong sexual appetites.

40  **languish** suffer feebly and passively.
**slow-chapped** slowly chewing.

42  **one ball** a cannon ball perhaps, but also the world of the lovers.

45–6  If time cannot be halted at least it can be made to pass rapidly since
they are enjoying themselves.

# Mourning

You, that decipher out the fate
Of human offsprings from the skies,
What mean these infants which of late
Spring from the stars of Clora's eyes?

Her eyes confused, and doubled o'er,                5
With tears suspended ere they flow,
Seem bending upwards, to restore
To heaven, whence it came, their woe.

When, moulding of the watery spheres,
Slow drops untie themselves away,                10
As if she, with those precious tears,
Would strow the ground where Strephon lay.

Yet some affirm, pretending art,
Her eyes have so her bosom drowned,
Only to soften near her heart                15
A place to fix another wound.

And, while vain pomp does her restrain
Within her solitary bower,
She courts herself in amorous rain;
Herself both Danaë and the shower.                    20

Nay, others, bolder, hence esteem
Joy now so much her master grown,
That whatsoever does but seem
Like grief, is from her windows thrown.

Nor that she pays, while she survives,                25
To her dead love this tribute due,
But casts abroad these donatives,
At the installing of a new.

How wide they dream! The Indian slaves
That dive for pearl through seas profound           30
Would find her tears yet deeper waves
And not of one the bottom sound.

I yet my silent judgement keep,
Disputing not what they believe:
But sure as oft as women weep,                        35
It is to be supposed they grieve.

1–2 **You ... skies**  You astrologers who cast horoscopes by studying the
     skies at the moment of a child's birth.

 3 **infants**  infant stars (tears which, like Clora's eyes, are shining
     globes) born 'from the stars of Clora's eyes'; 'infants' appears to refer
     back to 'offsprings', but these are stars, a means to predict the future
     rather than the subjects of such a prediction.

 5 Her eyes are seen distortedly through the tears which 'double' the
     eyes since they are the same shape.

 7 **bending**  looking.                                    7

12 **strow**  scatter.
    **Strephon**  typical pastoral name for the boy, as Clora is for the girl.

13 **some affirm**  The next two pairs of stanzas put forward alternative
     interpretations of Clora's behaviour, while the final pair hints at the
     poet's own 'silent judgement'.
    **pretending art**  laying claim to subtle knowledge.

16 **wound**  of love from Cupid's dart.

17  **vain pomp**  a meaningless outward show of mourning.

18  **bower**  lady's chamber.

19–20  Danaë was made pregnant by Jupiter who visited her in the form of a shower of golden rain. Here the accusation is of self-love.

22  **Joy**  at being rid of Strephon.

23–4  **That . . . thrown**  Anything suggestive of grief, such as tears, is thrown out of the 'windows' of her eyes.

27  **donatives**  largess, gifts to celebrate a special occasion.

29  **wide**  mistakenly.

31  **deeper**  It is impossible to fathom ('sound') or find out the meaning of her tears.

32  **sound**  a pun: not only 'to reach the bottom' but also 'safe or reliable'.

36  **It is to be supposed**  ambiguous: either, 'Women should be given the benefit of the doubt', or if 'supposed' is ironically stressed, 'You ought to think that women grieve even if we really know better.'

# The Definition of Love

My love is of a birth as rare
As 'tis for object strange and high:
It was begotten by Despair
Upon Impossibility.

Magnanimous Despair alone                                    5
Could show me so divine a thing,
Where feeble Hope could ne'er have flown
But vainly flapped its tinsel wing.

And yet I quickly might arrive
Where my extended soul is fixed,                             10
But Fate does iron wedges drive,
And always crowds itself betwixt.

For Fate with jealous eye does see
Two perfect loves, nor lets them close:
Their union would her ruin be,                               15
And her tyrannic power depose.

And therefore her decrees of steel
Us as the distant Poles have placed,
(Though Love's whole world on us doth wheel)
Not by themselves to be embraced,                                    20

Unless the giddy heavens fall,
And earth some new convulsion tear;
And, us to join, the world should all
Be cramped into a planisphere.

As lines (so loves) oblique may well                                 25
Themselves in every angle greet:
But ours so truly parallel,
Though infinite, can never meet.

Therefore the love which us doth bind,
But Fate so enviously debars,                                        30
Is the conjunction of the mind,
And opposition of the stars.

1–4  The poet's ideal love is by definition impossible and so can only be
     despaired of.

  5  **Magnanimous Despair** an oxymoron (placing together of apparently
     contradictory ideas) since 'magnanimous' means nobly courageous.

  8  **tinsel** cloth interwoven with gold or silver thread; hence something
     showy but insubstantial.

 10  His soul is unshakably directed ('fixed') towards the 'object' of his
     love.
     **extended** stretched out towards, strained; possibly its use as a
     geometrical term anticipates the imagery of stanza 7.

 14  **close** unite.

15–16  Fate would be powerless in the face of a perfect love. Compare the
     last two lines of Donne's 'The Good Morrow' (p40).

18–19  They are totally separated at the opposite poles, and yet their perfect
     love is the axis, running between the poles, on which 'Love's whole
     world' turns.

 24  **planisphere** the projection of a hemisphere onto a flat surface;
     Marvell has in mind a disk like the medal which commemorates
     Drake's circumnavigation of the globe. On one side is a map of the

northern hemisphere with the pole at the centre, and on the other a map of the southern hemisphere. Thus the two poles are brought together at the centre with only the thinness of the disk between them. This is the reverse of Donne's map image in 'Hymn to God my God', lines 13–15 (p71), for the planisphere appears to bring together that which must always remain 'poles apart', whereas the map appears to separate extreme east and extreme west which are in fact the same place.

25 **oblique** at an angle.

27–8 Again the perfect love ('parallel') can never, by definition, be fulfilled ('meet').

31 **conjunction** union (an ideal platonic love); also the coming together of two heavenly bodies in the same sign of the zodiac.

32 **opposition** hostility and the diametrically opposite positioning of two heavenly bodies (i.e. the opposite of 'conjunction').

# The Mower to the Glow-worms

Ye living lamps, by whose dear light
The nightingale does sit so late,
And studying all the summer night,
Her matchless songs does meditate;

Ye country comets, that portend                               5
No war, nor prince's funeral,
Shining unto no higher end
Than to presage the grass's fall;

Ye glow-worms, whose officious flame
To wandering mowers shows the way,                            10
That in the night have lost their aim,
And after foolish fires do stray;

Your courteous lights in vain you waste,
Since Juliana here is come,
For she my mind hath so displaced                             15
That I shall never find my home.

1 **living lamps** glow-worms.

5 **country comets** glow-worms again; comets were thought to foreshadow ('portend') serious matters, but these are simple/rural ('country') and have no greater purpose ('end') than to foretell ('presage') the hay harvest.

9 **officious** performing a kindly duty (not the modern meaning of meddlesome).

12 **foolish fires** a translation of 'ignes fatui', will-o'-the-wisps which were supposed to lead astray travellers who were lost at night; also the delusive fires of love.

# The Mower's Song

My mind was once the true survey
Of all these meadows fresh and gay,
And in the greenness of the grass
Did see its hopes as in a glass;
When Juliana came, and she                                    5
What I do to the grass, does to my thoughts and me.

But these, while I with sorrow pine,
Grew more luxuriant still and fine,
That not one blade of grass you spied,
But had a flower on either side;                              10
When Juliana came, and she
What I do to the grass, does to my thoughts and me.

Unthankful meadows, could you so
A fellowship so true forgo,
And in your gaudy May-games meet,                            15
While I lay trodden under feet?
When Juliana came, and she
What I do to the grass, does to my thoughts and me.

But what you in compassion ought,
Shall now by my revenge be wrought:                          20
And flowers, and grass, and I and all,
Will in one common ruin fall.
For Juliana comes, and she
What I do to the grass, does to my thoughts and me.

And thus, ye meadows, which have been                        25
Companions of my thoughts more green,
Shall now the heraldry become
With which I will adorn my tomb;
For Juliana comes, and she
What I do to the grass, does to my thoughts and me.          30

Ironically the Mower is himself cut down by Juliana's rejection of his
love. There are overtones of death; see the introductory note to
Herbert's 'Time' (p97).

1 **survey** picture.

3 **greenness** suggesting neither jealousy nor gullibility, but vigorous,
youthful optimism.

4 **glass** mirror.

7 **these** meadows.
**pine** waste away with grief.

9–10 **not one blade . . . But had** every blade had.

13 **so** in such a way.

14 **A fellowship . . . forgo** abandon so loyal a friendship (between
mower and meadows) . . .

15 **gaudy** brightly coloured; also perhaps joyful.

19 **ought** owed (as a debt of compassion).

20 **wrought** performed.

26 **green** Compare with line 3, but also with uses elsewhere, e.g. 'The
Garden', lines 18 and 48 (p114).

27 The fallen grass becomes the symbol of his own fall.

# The Picture of Little T. C.
# in a Prospect of Flowers

See with what simplicity
This nymph begins her golden days!
In the green grass she loves to lie,
And there with her fair aspect tames
The wilder flowers, and gives them names:                    5
But only with the roses plays;
        And them does tell
What colour best becomes them, and what smell.

Who can foretell for what high cause
This Darling of the Gods was born!                           10
Yet this is she whose chaster laws
The wanton Love shall one day fear,
And, under her command severe,
See his bow broke and ensigns torn.
        Happy, who can                                15
Appease this virtuous enemy of man!

O, then let me in time compound,
And parley with those conquering eyes;
Ere they have tried their force to wound,
Ere, with their glancing wheels, they drive                  20
In triumph over hearts that strive,
And them that yield but more despise.
        Let me be laid,
Where I may see thy glories from some shade.

Meantime, whilst every verdant thing                         25
Itself does at thy beauty charm,
Reform the errors of the spring;
Make that the tulips may have share
Of sweetness, seeing they are fair;
And roses of their thorns disarm:                            30
        But most procure
That violets may a longer age endure.

But, O young beauty of the woods,
Whom Nature courts with fruits and flowers,
Gather the flowers, but spare the buds;                      35
Lest Flora angry at thy crime,
To kill her infants in their prime,
Do quickly make the example yours;
           And, ere we see,
Nip in the blossom all our hopes and thee.                   40

**Little T. C.** probably Theophila ('Darling of the Gods') Cornwall
whose elder sister of the same name had died two days after baptism
('Whom the gods love dies young').

**Prospect** a setting both visual and mental.

4 **aspect** appearance.

12 **wanton Love** Cupid, who is both wilful and inconsiderate (the
normal meaning of 'wanton' when applied to children) and also
lascivious.

14 **ensigns** flags.

17 **compound** come to terms.

20 **glancing wheels** The image is of the conqueror's chariot with
perhaps a pun on 'glancing' = looking/striking a light blow.

25 **verdant** fresh green.

29 **sweetness** scent.

30 The rose can be a symbol of sexual love. Perhaps here T. C. is to
restore to love its innocence.

32 **violets** suggestive of innocence, but short-lived.

36 **Flora** goddess of flowers.

37 **prime** beginning.

40 **all our hopes** i.e. little T. C.

# The Garden

How vainly men themselves amaze
To win the palm, the oak, or bays,
And their uncessant labours see
Crowned from some single herb or tree,
Whose short and narrow vergèd shade                    5
Does prudently their toils upbraid,
While all flowers and all trees do close
To weave the garlands of repose.

Fair Quiet, have I found thee here,
And Innocence, thy sister dear!                        10
Mistaken long, I sought you then
In busy companies of men.
Your sacred plants, if here below,
Only among the plants will grow.
Society is all but rude,                               15
To this delicious solitude.

No white nor red was ever seen
So amorous as this lovely green.
Fond lovers, cruel as their flame,
Cut in these trees their mistress' name.               20
Little, alas, they know, or heed,
How far these beauties hers exceed!
Fair trees! wheresoe'er your barks I wound,
No name shall but your own be found.

When we have run our passion's heat,                   25
Love hither makes his best retreat.
The gods, that mortal beauty chase,
Still in a tree did end their race.
Apollo hunted Daphne so,
Only that she might laurel grow.                       30
And Pan did after Syrinx speed,
Not as a nymph, but for a reed.

What wondrous life is this I lead!
Ripe apples drop about my head;

The luscious clusters of the vine                               35
Upon my mouth do crush their wine;
The nectarine, and curious peach,
Into my hands themselves do reach;
Stumbling on melons, as I pass,
Ensnared with flowers, I fall on grass.                         40

Meanwhile the mind, from pleasures less,
Withdraws into its happiness:
The mind, that ocean where each kind
Does straight its own resemblance find;
Yet it creates, transcending these,                             45
Far other worlds, and other seas,
Annihilating all that's made
To a green thought in a green shade.

Here at the fountain's sliding foot,
Or at some fruit-tree's mossy root,                             50
Casting the body's vest aside,
My soul into the boughs does glide:
There like a bird it sits, and sings,
Then whets, and combs its silver wings;
And, till prepared for longer flight,                           55
Waves in its plumes the various light.

Such was that happy garden-state,
While man there walked without a mate:
After a place so pure, and sweet,
What other help could yet be meet!                              60
But 'twas beyond a mortal's share
To wander solitary there:
Two paradises 'twere in one
To live in paradise alone.

How well the skilful gardener drew                              65
Of flowers and herbs this dial new,
Where from above the milder sun
Does through a fragrant zodiac run;
And, as it works, the industrious bee
Computes its time as well as we.                                70

How could such sweet and wholesome hours
Be reckoned but with herbs and flowers!

1   **vainly** pointlessly and conceitedly.
    **amaze** drive to their wits' end.

2   triumphal wreaths for the victor, the ruler and the poet respectively.

5   **vergèd shade** surrounding shadow.

6   **toils** labours or strife, but also nets used to snare animals.
    **upbraid** rebuke, but also 'braid up' hair in a wreath or perhaps set
    up a snare. The whole line is deliberately ambiguous.

7   **close** unite.

13–14 **Your sacred . . . grow** If Quiet and Innocence flourish anywhere it is
    among the plants.

15  **Society . . . rude** Human company is almost uncouth; a reversal of
    the normal contempt for rustic life.

17  **white nor red** woman's beauty.

18  **amorous** lovable.

19  **Fond** loving and foolish.
    **flame** passion.

22  **these beauties** i.e. of the trees.

23  **wound** by carving names.

25  **When . . . heat** When our passion is exhausted . . .

28  **Still** always.

29–32 Daphne and Syrinx both turned into plants to escape rape. Marvell
    suggests that the pursuit was *in order to* turn them into plants of
    'lovely green'. (Daphne's laurel or bay-tree provides the 'bays' of line
    2 to reward the poet; Apollo was the god of poetic inspiration. From
    Syrinx's reed were made the pan-pipes which accompany pastoral
    song.)

37  **nectarine** type of peach.
    **curious** exquisite.

40  **fall** One of a number of hints in this stanza not only of Paradise, but
    of man's fall and expulsion from it.

41  **pleasures less** lesser pleasures.

43–6 The ocean was thought to contain the equivalent of every kind of life
    on land. Similarly the mind contains the platonic idea or ideal
    concept of everything that exists (see introduction, p4). The mind,

going beyond ('transcending') real things, can create whole new worlds by use of the imagination.

47 **Annihilating . . . made** reducing the whole of creation . . .

51 **vest** clothing; the body clothes the soul.

54 **whets** preens.

55 **longer flight** at death?

56 **various light** varying colours.

57–8 Adam in the Garden of Eden before the creation of Eve.

60 **meet** appropriate; in the Bible Eve was the 'help meet for' Adam (Genesis 2.18, 20).

61 **But . . . share** It was too great a blessing for any human . . .

66 **dial** The garden is perhaps laid out in the form of a sun-dial. The changes in the garden in any case make clear the changing seasons.

67 **milder** shining through leaves?

68 In a year the sun passes through each sign of the zodiac. Here it sees each seasonal change in the garden.

70 **time** pun on thyme, a herb much liked by bees.

71 **hours** spent in the garden.

72 **but** except.

# Bermudas

Where the remote Bermudas ride
In the ocean's bosom unespied,
From a small boat, that rowed along,
The listening winds received this song:
 What should we do but sing his praise    5
That led us through the watery maze,
Unto an isle so long unknown,
And yet far kinder than our own?
Where he the huge sea-monsters wracks,
That lift the deep upon their backs,     10
He lands us on a grassy stage,
Safe from the storms, and prelate's rage.

He gave us this eternal spring,
Which here enamels everything,
And sends the fowl to us in care,                               15
On daily visits through the air.
He hangs in shades the orange bright,
Like golden lamps in a green night,
And does in the pom'granates close
Jewels more rich than Ormus shows.                              20
He makes the figs our mouths to meet,
And throws the melons at our feet,
But apples plants of such a price
No tree could ever bear them twice.
With cedars, chosen by his hand,                                25
From Lebanon, he stores the land,
And makes the hollow seas, that roar,
Proclaim the ambergris on shore.
He cast (of which we rather boast)
The gospel's pearl upon our coast,                              30
And in these rocks for us did frame
A temple, where to sound his name.
Oh let our voice his praise exalt,
Till it arrive at heaven's vault:
Which thence (perhaps) rebounding, may                          35
Echo beyond the Mexique Bay.
      Thus sung they, in the English boat,
An holy and a cheerful note,
And all the way, to guide their chime,
With falling oars they kept the time.                           40

This was presumably written sometime after July 1653 when Marvell
stayed with John Oxenbridge, a Puritan clergyman and fellow of
Eton College who went to the Bermudas after being persecuted by
Archbishop Laud in 1634.

1  **ride** like a boat at anchor.

7  not discovered until 1515.

8  **far kinder** in the richness of its fruits and the lack of persecution.

12  **prelate** important churchman (presumably Laud).

14  **enamels** decorates with bright colours.

20 **Ormus** Hormus in the Persian Gulf, the centre of the trade in pearls
with India.

23 **apples** pineapples.

24 The pineapple is not a tree at all, but a low-growing plant which is
cut down when its single fruit is reaped.

26 **stores** stocks.

28 **Proclaim** make known.
**ambergris** a wax-like substance found floating in tropical seas,
secreted by unhealthy sperm whales and used in perfumes and
cookery; considered valuable.

29 **rather** more fittingly, more willingly.

30 **gospel's pearl** the precious truth of Christianity.

31 **frame** construct.

32 **sound** praise aloud.


# The Coronet

When for the thorns with which I long, too long,
   With many a piercing wound,
   My Saviour's head have crowned,
I seek with garlands to redress that wrong:
   Through every garden, every mead,         5
I gather flowers (my fruits are only flowers),
   Dismantling all the fragrant towers
That once adorned my shepherdess's head.
And now when I have summed up all my store,
   Thinking (so I myself deceive)         10
   So rich a chaplet thence to weave
As never yet the King of Glory wore:
   Alas, I find the serpent old
   That, twining in his speckled breast,
   About the flowers disguised does fold,      15
   With wreaths of fame and interest.
Ah, foolish man, that wouldst debase with them,
And mortal glory, Heaven's diadem!
But Thou who only couldst the serpent tame,

Either his slippery knots at once untie;                    20
And disentangle all his winding snare;
Or shatter too with him my curious frame,
And let these wither, so that he may die,
Though set with skill and chosen out with care:
That they, while Thou on both their spoils dost tread,      25
May crown thy feet, that could not crown thy head.

1–3 Since Christ died to save all men from their sins, all those who sin
contribute to his suffering. At His trial 'when they had plaited a
crown of thorns, they put it upon his head . . . and they bowed the
knee before him, and mocked him, saying, Hail, King of the Jews!'
(Matthew 27.29).

4 The 'garland' with which he wishes to put right ('redress') the wrong
is perhaps his poetry, no longer directed to praising his mistress, but
his God.

7 **towers** elaborate head-dresses.

9 **summed up all my store** gathered together all that I possess.

11 **chaplet** coronet.

13 **serpent** devil; as in the Garden of Eden, the serpent ruins the pastoral
delights.

15 **fold** entwine itself.

16 **interest** self-interest.

17 **them** 'fame and interest'.

18 **mortal** human and soon dead.

19 **Thou who only** Christ who alone. . .

20 **slippery** slimy and deceitful.

21 **winding** twisting and enticing.

22 **Or shatter . . . frame** or destroy the elaborate structure ('curious
frame') of my coronet at the same time as destroying him (the
serpent).

23 **these** the flowers.
**so that** so long as.

24 **Though . . . care** although the flowers were carefully chosen and
placed in the wreath with care.

25 **spoils** booty, but also the sloughed skin of a snake. Compare the
words of the Litany: 'That it may please thee . . . to beat down Satan
under our feet.'

# Clorinda and Damon

c: Damon, come drive thy flocks this way.
d: No, 'tis too late; they went astray.
c: I have a grassy scutcheon spied,
    Where Flora blazons all her pride.
    The grass I aim to feast thy sheep:                    5
    The flowers I for thy temples keep.
d: Grass withers; and the flowers too fade.
c: Seize the short joys then, ere they vade.
    Seest thou that unfrequented cave?
d: That den?                                               10
c:                 Love's Shrine.
d:                               But virtue's grave.
c: In whose cool bosom we may lie
    Safe from the sun.
d:                         Not heaven's eye.
c: Near this, a fountain's liquid bell
    Tinkles within the concave shell.
d: Might a soul bathe there and be clean,                 15
    Or slake its drought?
c:                           What is't you mean?
d: These once had been enticing things,
    Clorinda, pastures, caves, and springs.
c: And what late change?
d:                           The other day
    Pan met me.                                           20
c:              What did great Pan say?
d: Words that transcend poor shepherds' skill,
    But he e'er since my songs does fill:
    And his name swells my slender oat.
c: Sweet must Pan sound in Damon's note.
d: Clorinda's voice might make it sweet.                  25
c: Who would not in Pan's praises meet?
CHORUS
Of Pan the flowery pastures sing,
Caves echo, and the fountains ring.
Sing then while he doth us inspire;
For all the world is our Pan's choir.                     30

The pastoral dialogue between nymph and shepherd has been christianised. Pan has become another name for Christ.

2    'All we like sheep have gone astray [sinned]' (Isaiah 53.6).

3–4    Flora, the goddess of flowers, depicts her heraldic bearings in flowers on a shield of grass.

7    'All flesh is grass, and all the goodliness thereof is as the flower of the field: The grass withereth, the flower fadeth' (Isaiah 40.6,7).

8    **ere they vade**  before they go; the argument is that of 'To His Coy Mistress' (p103).

12    The sun is often called 'heaven's eye', but Damon has God in mind.

15–16    A reference to baptism and to Jesus's saying to the woman of Samaria: 'the water that I shall give . . . shall be . . . a well of water springing up into everlasting life' (John 4.14).

21    **transcend**  are beyond.

22    **does fill**  is all the subject matter of my songs.

23    **oat**  pipe made from an oat straw.

# A Dialogue between the Soul and Body

*Soul*
O, who shall from this dungeon raise
A soul, enslaved so many ways,
With bolts of bones, that fettered stands
In feet, and manacled in hands;
Here blinded with an eye; and there                    5
Deaf with the drumming of an ear;
A soul hung up, as 'twere, in chains
Of nerves, and arteries, and veins;
Tortured, besides each other part,
In a vain head, and double heart?                    10

*Body*
O, who shall me deliver whole,
From bonds of this tyrannic soul,
Which, stretched upright, impales me so,
That mine own precipice I go;
And warms and moves this needless frame                    15

(A fever could but do the same);
And, wanting where its spite to try,
Has made me live to let me die;
A body that could never rest,
Since this ill spirit it possessed?

*Soul*                                                     20
What magic could me thus confine
Within another's grief to pine,
Where, whatsoever it complain,
I feel, that cannot feel, the pain;
And all my care itself employs,                           25
That to preserve, which me destroys;
Constrained not only to endure
Diseases, but, what's worse, the cure;
And ready oft the port to gain,
Am shipwrecked into health again?                         30

*Body*
But physic yet could never reach
The maladies thou me dost teach:
Whom first the cramp of hope does tear,
And then the palsy shakes of fear;
The pestilence of love does heat,                         35
Or hatred's hidden ulcer eat;
Joy's cheerful madness does perplex,
Or sorrow's other madness vex;
Which knowledge forces me to know,
And memory will not forgo.                                40
What but a soul could have the wit
To build me up for sin so fit?
So architects do square and hew
Green trees that in the forest grew.

---

 1 **this dungeon** the body, as is made clear in lines 3 and 4.
5–6 Paradoxically the senses are confusing rather than enlightening.
 7 **hung . . . in chains** as a tortured prisoner.
10 **vain** foolish, arrogant; also empty.
    **double** treacherous; also over-full (of emotions).
12 **bonds** chains.

13 **impales** goes through like a spike or fences in.

14 The soul brings the body to life and makes it walk upright so that it is in danger of falling (not least in the moral sense).

15 **needless frame** body that needs nothing.

17 **And . . . to try** and lacking any other target for its spite . . .

20 **possessed** not simply 'owned'; the soul's animation of the body is compared to possession by an evil spirit ('it' can be either subject or object).

22 **pine** fade away with grief.

23-4 The soul cannot feel physical pain and yet suffers if the body does.

26 **That . . . which me destroys** i.e. the body.

27 **Constrained** forced.

28-30 The soul is eager to be released from the body by death and gain the 'port' of heaven.

31 **physic** medicine.

34 **the palsy . . . fear** the palsy of fear shakes me.

35 **pestilence** plague.

40 **forgo** release.

41-4 These last four lines do not fit into the pattern of the poem and there is some doubt as to whether the poem is complete. The unresolved argument, although quite unlike the conclusion of the previous dialogue poem, could be seen as typical of Marvell, nonetheless, in its fierce irony (compare Marvell's use elsewhere of 'green' imagery) and in the poet's own detachment.


# On a Drop of Dew

See how the orient dew,
Shed from the bosom of the morn
   Into the blowing roses,
Yet careless of its mansion new,
For the clear region where 'twas born      5
    Round in itself incloses:
    And in its little globe's extent,
Frames as it can its native element;

How it the purple flower does slight,
   Scarce touching where it lies,             10
But gazing back upon the skies,
   Shines with a mournful light,
     Like its own tear,
Because so long divided from the sphere.
   Restless it rolls and unsecure,        15
    Trembling lest it grow impure,
   Till the warm sun pity its pain,
And to the skies exhale it back again.
    So the soul, that drop, that ray
Of the clear fountain of eternal day,      20
Could it within the human flower be seen,
   Remembering still its former height,
   Shuns the sweet leaves and blossoms green,
   And recollecting its own light,
Does, in its pure and circling thoughts, express   25
The greater heaven in an heaven less.
   In how coy a figure wound,
   Every way it turns away:
   So the world excluding round,
   Yet receiving in the day,        30
   Dark beneath, but bright above,
   Here disdaining, there in love.
   How loose and easy hence to go,
   How girt and ready to ascend,
   Moving but on a point below,      35
   It all about does upwards bend.
Such did the manna's sacred dew distill,
White and entire, though congealed and chill,
Congealed on earth: but does, dissolving, run
Into the glories of the almighty sun.      40

The poem is an extended comparison of the soul to a drop of dew.
Both have fallen from heaven and long to return there. Compare
Vaughan's 'The Retreat' (p150).

1 **orient** bright (like a pearl from the orient).

3 **blowing** blossoming.

4 **careless** heedless.
**mansion** resting place.

5–6 The dew drop contains within itself a sparkling light which is the essential quality of heaven, 'that clear (i.e. bright) region' where it was formed.

7–8 The spherical dew drop re-creates in miniature the sphere of the sky ('element') which is its appropriate setting ('element') where it was born.

9 **purple** suggests both splendour and sin.
**slight** scornfully neglect.

14 **sphere** of heaven.

18 **exhale** draw up as vapour.

21 **human flower** the body.

23 the attractions of earth.

24 **recollecting** gathering again *and* remembering.

25–6 Just as the drop of dew is a model of the heaven from which it came (lines 5–8), so is the soul.

27–8 Just as the sphere only touches at a single point and curves away up towards heaven (as in lines 9–10), so the 'coy' soul turns away from the sins of the world towards God.

29–32 The self-contained sphere of the soul excludes 'the world' (that is 'worldly' as opposed to heavenly concerns), but it lets in the bright light of day. Underneath it is the darkness of this world ('Here') which it disdains, but above is the brightness of heaven ('there') which it loves.

34 **girt** ready to go; literally: with loose clothes drawn up within a belt for unimpeded movement. The Jews ate the Passover with 'loins girded' before setting out on the exodus (Exodus 12.11) and Christ uses the same image when telling his disciples that they must be ready to face God (Luke 12.35).

35–6 as in lines 27–8.

37 **manna** the miraculous food with which the Jews were fed during the exodus, which came from heaven like dew: 'And when the dew that lay was gone up, behold, upon the face of the wilderness there lay a small round thing, as small as the hoar frost on the ground . . . And they gathered it every morning, every man according to his eating: and when the sun waxed hot, it melted.' (Exodus 16.14, 21).

39–40 The soul, freed from the body, is drawn back to God.

# An Horatian Ode upon Cromwell's Return from Ireland

The forward youth that would appear
Must now forsake his muses dear,
   Nor in the shadows sing
   His numbers languishing.
'Tis time to leave the books in dust,            5
And oil the unusèd armour's rust:
   Removing from the wall
   The corslet of the hall.
So restless Cromwell could not cease
In the inglorious arts of peace,            10
   But through adventurous war
   Urgèd his active star.
And, like the three-forked lightning, first
Breaking the clouds where it was nursed,
   Did thorough his own side            15
   His fiery way divide.
For 'tis all one to courage high
The emulous or enemy:
   And with such to inclose
   Is more than to oppose.            20
Then burning through the air he went,
And palaces and temples rent:
   And Caesar's head at last
   Did through his laurels blast.
'Tis madness to resist or blame            25
The force of angry heaven's flame:
   And, if we would speak true,
   Much to the man is due,
Who, from his private gardens, where
He lived reservèd and austere,            30
   As if his highest plot
   To plant the bergamot,
Could by industrious valour climb
To ruin the great work of time,

And cast the kingdoms old                          35
  Into another mould,
Though justice against fate complain,
And plead the ancient rights in vain:
    But those do hold or break
    As men are strong or weak.                40
Nature, that hateth emptiness,
Allows of penetration less:
    And therefore must make room
    Where greater spirits come.
What field of all the Civil Wars,                  45
Where his were not the deepest scars?
    And Hampton shows what part
    He had of wiser art,
Where, twining subtle fears with hope,
He wove a net of such a scope,                     50
    That Charles himself might chase
    To Carisbrooke's narrow case:
That thence the royal actor born
The tragic scaffold might adorn:
    While round the armèd bands              55
    Did clap their bloody hands.
*He* nothing common did or mean
Upon that memorable scene:
    But with his keener eye
    The axe's edge did try:                  60
Nor called the gods with vulgar spite
To vindicate his helpless right,
    But bowed his comely head,
    Down, as upon a bed.
This was that memorable hour                       65
Which first assured the forcèd power.
    So when they did design
    The Capitol's first line,
A bleeding head where they begun,
Did fright the architects to run;                  70
    And yet in that the State
    Foresaw its happy fate.

And now the Irish are ashamed
To see themselves in one year tamed:
   So much one man can do,               75
   That does both act and know.
They can affirm his praises best,
And have, though overcome, confessed
   How good he is, how just,
   And fit for highest trust:             80
Nor yet grown stiffer with command,
But still in the Republic's hand:
   How fit he is to sway
   That can so well obey.
He to the Commons' feet presents        85
A kingdom, for his first year's rents:
   And, what he may, forbears
   His fame, to make it theirs:
And has his sword and spoils ungirt,
To lay them at the public's skirt.        90
   So when the falcon high
   Falls heavy from the sky,
She, having killed, no more does search
But on the next green bough to perch,
   Where, when he first does lure,     95
   The falconer has her sure.
What may not then our isle presume
While Victory his crest does plume?
   What may not others fear
   If thus he crowns each year?     100
A Caesar, he, ere long to Gaul,
To Italy an Hannibal,
   And to all states not free
   Shall climacteric be.
The Pict no shelter now shall find     105
Within his parti-coloured mind,
   But from this valour sad
   Shrink underneath the plaid:
Happy, if in the tufted brake
The English hunter him mistake,     110

Nor lay his hounds in near
The Caledonian deer.
But thou, the Wars' and Fortune's son,
March indefatigably on,
   And for the last effect              115
   Still keep thy sword erect:
Besides the force it has to fright
The spirits of the shady night,
   The same arts that did gain
   A power, must it maintain.           120

Cromwell returned from Ireland in May 1650 and took command of
the army to invade Scotland in June on the resignation of General
Fairfax (by whom Marvell was later employed as a tutor). The
invasion began on 22 July. The Roman poet Horace addressed a
number of his Odes to the emperor Augustus who, like Cromwell,
had both triumphed in civil war and defeated his country's enemies.

1 **forward** ambitious, or presumptuous.
  **appear** win reputation.

2 **muses** goddesses of artistic inspiration.

4 **numbers languishing** melancholy love poems.

8 **corslet** armour protecting the trunk.

9 **cease** refrain from action.

12 Cromwell is no passive victim of fate but takes his fortune into his
own hands.

13–16 **like the . . . divide** As the lightning breaks through the cloud in
which it was formed so he forced his way above his rivals in the
Parliamentary party.

18 **The emulous** jealous rivals.

19–20 If 'such' refers to 'the emulous' then the rest of the couplet may mean
'to contain and control is better than to fight' (possibly a reference to
Cromwell's growing influence). If 'such' refers to 'courage high' then
perhaps it means 'to hinder such a man is more difficult for his
enemies/frustrating to him, than to oppose him in battle'.

23–4 Caesar's laurel wreath is Charles's crown. Supposedly the laurel
could not be struck by lightning (here an image for Cromwell) just as
the crown was above the people, but Charles I was executed on 30
January 1649.

26 **angry heaven's flame** both lightning and Cromwell.

32 **bergamot** type of pear tree.

38 **the ancient rights** of the overthrown monarchy.

41–2 **Nature . . . less** Nature abhors a vacuum, but still less does she allow two objects to occupy the same space. (Charles must 'make room' for Cromwell.)

46 **scars** not only Cromwell's actual wound at Marston Moor, but the 'scars' of anxiety.

47–52 Marvell supports the now discredited view that Cromwell used his 'wiser art' to trick Charles into fleeing from custody at Hampton Court to the narrow confines ('case') of Carisbrooke Castle where he was betrayed to the governor.

54 **scaffold** on which Charles was executed.

59 **keener** sharper (than the axe).

60 **try** test.

62 **vindicate** defend.

63 **comely** suggests kingly dignity rather than physical beauty.

66 **which first . . . power** which first firmly established the power that had been taken by force.

67–72 The discovery of a human head when the foundations of Jupiter's temple on the Capitol were being dug was taken as a good omen for the future of the state. Charles's death, although horrifying, is a good omen for England under Cromwell.

77 **They** the Irish. There is no hint in the following lines of Cromwell's ruthless violence.

82 **still** always.

83 **sway** command.

84 Cromwell did not become Lord Protector until 1653.

87 **forbears** does not insist upon; Cromwell gives the credit to Parliament.

89–90 **And has . . . skirt** He has laid aside ('ungirt') his power and the spoils of war to put them at the feet of the state.

91–6 Cromwell is the falcon and Parliament the falconer. To 'lure' (line 95) is to recapture the hawk after it has killed, with a device made of feathers (through which the hawk is fed while in training) attached to a thong.

101–2 **A Caesar . . . Hannibal** He will soon be the invader of France and of Italy.

104 **climacteric** introducing a new era; stress third syllable.

105 **Pict** Scot; with a pun on the Latin 'pictum' meaning painted linking with 'parti-coloured'; 'parti-' also suggests political factions.

107 **sad** steadfast.

108 **plaid** The tartan cloth will provide protective colouring.

109 **brake** clump of bushes.

111 **lay in** send hounds into a covert.

112 **Caledonian deer** the pursued Scot.

115 **effect** achievement.

117–8 The reversed sword makes the sign of the cross.

119–20 The military skills that won power must also defend it.

# Henry Vaughan
## 1621–1695

## To Amoret, of the Difference 'Twixt Him, and Other Lovers, and what True Love is

Mark, when the Evening's cooler wings
    Fan the afflicted air, how the faint Sun,
        Leaving undone,
        What he begun,
Those spurious flames sucked up from slime, and earth    5
        To their first, low birth,
        Resigns, and brings.

They shoot their tinsel beams, and vanities,
    Threading with those false fires their way;
        But as you stay    10
        And see them stray,
You lose the flaming track, and subtly they
        Languish away,
        And cheat your eyes.

Just so base, sublunary lovers' hearts    15
    Fed on loose profane desires,
        May for an eye,
        Or face comply:
But those removed, they will as soon depart,
        And show their art,    20
        And painted fires.

Whilst I by powerful love, so much refined,
    That my absent soul the same is,
        Careless to miss,
        A glance, or kiss,    25

Can with those elements of lust and sense,
  Freely dispense,
  And court the mind.

Thus to the north the loadstones move,
  And thus to them the enamoured steel aspires:    30
   Thus, *Amoret*,
   I do affect;
And thus by wingèd beams, and mutual fire,
  Spirits and stars conspire,
  And this is LOVE.         35

There are six poems addressed to Amoret in Vaughan's first volume of poetry (published 1646). She was perhaps his first wife, Catherine Wise. This poem is clearly influenced by Donne's 'A Valediction forbidding Mourning' in its treatment of platonic 'True Love' and contains a number of verbal echoes of Donne's poem (p51). The image of the 'spurious flames' has been explained in terms of the sunset or the will-o'-the-wisp (*ignis fatuus*), but given Vaughan's interest in meteors or shooting stars it seems most probable that it is these that he has in mind (see Rudrum's edition of Vaughan's poems pp452–3).

 1 **Mark** notice.

 2 **afflicted** by the heat; it is in August that meteors are most often seen.
  **faint** weary.

5–7 **Those spurious . . . brings** The sun returns those counterfeit flames which it has sucked up from the slime and earth, sending them back to their lowly place of origin.

 8 The attractiveness of the meteors is flashy ('tinsel') and worthless ('vanities').

13 **Languish** fade.

15 **sublunary** see note on line 13 of Donne's 'Valediction' (p53).

15–21 The love of sublunary Lovers originates in immoral and impious ('loose profane') desires just as the 'spurious flames' come from 'slime and earth'. In the absence of physical attractions their supposedly loving hearts reveal their trickery ('show their art') and false passion ('painted' suggests here the false beauty of make-up).

23 **That my . . . is** that my soul is unaffected by absence . . .

26 **elements** component parts. The poet can dispense with the sexual attractions that make up a baser love and concentrate on a platonic union of minds.

29 **loadstones** magnetic oxide of iron used in compasses and as magnets.

30 The use of 'enamoured' stresses the platonist theory that attraction or love is a universal principle. Magnetism links 'loadstones' and 'steel'; 'winged beams' the 'Spirits'; 'mutual fire' the 'stars'; and love, Amoret and the poet. All these links which, unlike lust, do not depend on physical contact are different aspects of LOVE.

32 **affect** aim towards *and* feel affection.

34 **conspire** agree or act in harmony.

# To Amoret, Walking in a Starry Evening

If *Amoret*, that glorious eye,
    In the first birth of light,
      And death of night,
Had with those elder fires you spy
    Scattered so high         5
      Receivèd form, and sight;

We might suspect in the vast Ring,
    Amidst these golden glories,
      And fiery stories;
Whether the Sun had been the King,      10
    And guide of Day,
      Or your brighter eye should sway;

But, *Amoret*, such is my fate,
    That if thy face a Star
      Had shined from far,        15
I am persuaded in that state
    'Twixt thee, and me,
      Of some predestined sympathy.

For sure such two conspiring minds,
    Which no accident, or sight,          20
        Did thus unite;
Whom no distance can confine,
      Start, or decline,
One, for another, were designed.

1 **eye** Amoret's eye.

2 At the beginning of Creation when God said: 'Let there be light' (Genesis 1.3).

4 **elder fires** the stars created before Amoret's eye.

7 **suspect** doubt (whether the sun or Amoret's eye would have been the king of the heavenly bodies).
**vast Ring** the universe.

9 **stories** legends, or the different levels of the Ptolemaic universe (crystal spheres supposedly revolved around the earth at different heights supporting the heavenly bodies).

12 **sway** rule.

18 **sympathy** affinity; the word is also used for the attraction between iron and loadstone (see previous poem).

19 **conspiring** acting in harmony.

20 **accident** non-essential quality.
**sight** outward appearance.

22 **confine** separate.

23 **Start** displace.
**decline** turn aside.

24 The platonic union of their minds, regardless of externals and unaffected by physical separation, proves that they were 'designed' for each other, that their 'sympathy' was 'predestined'.


# Anguish

My God and King! to thee
    I bow my knee,
I bow my troubled soul, and greet
With my foul heart thy holy feet.

Cast it, or tread it! It shall do 5
Ev'n what thou wilt, and praise thee too.

My God, could I weep blood,
Gladly I would;
Or if thou wilt give me that art,
Which through the eyes pours out the heart, 10
I will exhaust it all, and make
Myself all tears, a weeping lake.

O! 'tis an easy thing
To write and sing;
But to write true, unfeignèd verse 15
Is very hard! O God, disperse
These weights, and give my spirit leave
To act as well as to conceive!

O my God, hear my cry;
Or let me die! – 20

5 **Cast** spurn aside.
9 **art** skill.
15 **unfeignèd** sincere.
15–16 Compare Herbert's 'Jordan (2)' (p89).
17 Compare 'let us lay aside every weight, and the sin which doth so
easily beset us' (Hebrews 12.1).
18 **conceive** think of an idea.

# 'Joy of my life! while left me here'
¶

Joy of my life! while left me here,
And still my love!
How in thy absence thou dost steer
Me from above!
A life well led 5
This truth commends,
With quick, or dead
It never ends.

Stars are of mighty use: the night
     Is dark, and long;            10
The road foul, and where one goes right,
     Six may go wrong.
     One twinkling ray
     Shot o'er some cloud,
     May clear much way       15
     And guide a crowd.

God's saints are shining lights: who stays
     Here long must pass
O'er dark hills, swift streams, and steep ways
     As smooth as glass;      20
     But these all night
     Like candles, shed
     Their beams, and light
     Us into bed.

They are (indeed) our pillar-fires     25
     Seen as we go:
They are that City's shining spires
     We travel to;
     A swordlike gleam
     Kept man for sin      30
     First *out*; this beam
     Will guide him *in*.

There are nine poems in *Silex Scintillans* with no title but merely a paragraph mark above them. They are a response to the death of those close to Vaughan, particularly his younger brother William (died 1648), but this poem may commemorate the death of his first wife, Elizabeth.

7 **quick** living.

18 **Here** in this world.

24 **bed** safety and comfort at the end of life's day.

25 **pillar-fires** like the guidance God gave to Moses and the Jews: 'And the Lord went before them by day in a pillar of a cloud, to lead them the way; and by night in a pillar of fire, to give them light' (Exodus 13.21).

27 **that City** St John the Divine has a vision of 'the holy city, new
Jerusalem, coming down from God out of heaven'. Its 'light was like
unto a stone most precious, even like a jasper stone, clear as crystal'
(Revelation 21.2 and 11).

)–31 When Adam and Eve were driven out of the Garden of Eden for
disobedience they were prevented from returning by Cherubim and 'a
flaming sword which turned every way' (Genesis 3.24).

# Man

Weighing the steadfastness and state
Of some mean things which here below reside,
Where birds like watchful clocks the noiseless date
And intercourse of times divide,
Where bees at night get home and hive, and flowers          5
Early, as well as late,
Rise with the sun, and set in the same bowers;

I would (said I) my God would give
The staidness of these things to man! for these
To his divine appointments ever cleave,                    10
And no new business breaks their peace;
The birds nor sow, nor reap, yet sup and dine,
The flowers without clothes live,
Yet *Solomon* was never dressed so fine.

Man hath still either toys, or care;                       15
He hath no root, nor to one place is tied,
But ever restless and irregular
About this earth doth run and ride;
He knows he hath a home, but scarce knows where,
He says it is so far                                       20
That he hath quite forgot how to go there.

He knocks at all doors, strays and roams,
Nay hath not so much wit as some stones have
Which in the darkest nights point to their homes,
By some hid sense their Maker gave;                        25

Man is the shuttle, to whose winding quest
        And passage through these looms
God ordered motion, but ordained no rest.

1   **state** stable condition; the regularity of the natural order, albeit in the humbler aspects of creation ('mean things'), provides an example which man fails to follow.

8   **I would** I wish.

9   **staidness** constancy.

10   **To his . . . cleave** always follow God's decrees exactly . . .

12–14   Christ urged his listeners to take no thought for worldly things: 'Behold the fowls of the air: for they sow not, neither do they reap, nor gather into barns; yet your heavenly Father feedeth them . . . Consider the lilies of the field, how they grow; they toil not, neither do they spin: And yet I say unto you, That even Solomon in all his glory was not arrayed like one of these' (Matthew 6.26, 28–9).

15   **toys** idle fancies.

23   **some stones** loadstones (used in early compasses).

26   **shuttle** part of the loom in perpetual movement carrying the weft thread across between the warp threads.

28   Compare the conclusion of Herbert's 'The Pulley' (p94).

# The Morning-Watch

O joys! Infinite sweetness! with what flowers,
And shoots of glory, my soul breaks and buds!
        All the long hours
        Of night, and rest
        Through the still shrouds       5
        Of sleep, and clouds,
      This dew fell on my breast;
        O how it *bloods*,
And *spirits* all my earth! hark! In what rings,
And *hymning circulations* the quick world    10
        Awakes, and sings;
        The rising winds,

And falling springs,
Birds, beasts, all things
Adore him in their kinds.                                    15
Thus all is hurled
In sacred *hymns*, and *order*, the great *chime*
And *symphony* of nature. Prayer is
The world in tune,
A spirit-voice,                                             20
And vocal joys
Whose *echo is* heaven's bliss.
O let me climb
When I lie down! The pious soul by night
Is like a clouded star, whose beams though said            25
To shed their light
Under some cloud
Yet are above,
And shine, and move
Beyond that misty shroud.                                  30
So in my bed
That curtained grave, though sleep, like ashes, hide
My lamp, and life, both shall in thee abide.

**The Morning-Watch** the last hours before morning; also watch in
the sense of a religious exercise. Both meanings are perhaps
suggested in the Authorised Version's translation of verse 6 of Psalm
130: 'My soul waiteth for the Lord More than they that watch for the
morning.' Coverdale's translation is: 'My soul fleeth unto the Lord:
before the morning watch, I say, before the morning watch.'

7 Part of Isaac's blessing to Jacob is the 'dew of heaven' and elsewhere
it is an image of God's love: 'I will be as the dew unto Israel: he shall
grow as the lily, and cast forth his roots as Lebanon' (Hosea 14.5).

8–9 **O how . . . earth** O how it gives full life to my body! The 'earth' of
his body is a microcosm of the whole world newly awoken to life.
Spirits are the refined and animating substances supposedly carried in
the blood; here the word is used as a verb.

10 The life-giving circulation of the blood is reflected in the movements
of the living ('quick') world which sings praise to its Creator.

15 **in their kinds** according to their natures.

16 **hurled** whirled.

17–18  **chime And symphony** Both words mean harmony both literally and metaphorically. Compare the end of 'Denial' (p82).

23  **climb** in prayer.

24–33  Just as the star hidden by cloud is still shining above, so the 'pious soul' shrouded by sleep can still climb above and abide in God.

# The Evening-Watch

*A Dialogue*

*Body*

> Farewell! I go to sleep; but when
> The day-star springs, I'll wake again.

*Soul*

> Go, sleep in peace; and when thou liest
> Unnumbered in thy dust, when all this frame
> Is but one dram, and what thou now descriest    5
> In several parts shall want a name,
> Then may his peace be with thee, and each dust
> Writ in his book, who ne'er betrayed man's trust!

*Body*

> Amen! but hark, ere we two stray,
> How many hours dost think 'till day?    10

*Soul*

> Ah! go; thou art weak, and sleepy. Heaven
> Is a plain watch, and without figures winds
> All ages up; who drew this circle even
> He fills it; days, and hours are *blinds.*
> Yet, this take with thee; the last gasp of time    15
> Is thy first breath, and man's *eternal prime.*

1  **sleep** the sleep of death, just as the 'evening' is the evening of life.

1–2  **when The day-star springs** at the second coming of Christ, who is 'the bright and morning star' (Revelation 22.16); see also II Peter 1.19: 'until the day dawn, and the day star arise in your hearts'.

4 **unnumbered** unnoted.
**frame** of the body.

5 **descriest** see.

6 **want** lack.

8 **his book** Christ's book of judgement.

9 **stray** separate (at death).

10 **day** resurrection at the coming of the 'day star'.

12 **plain watch** clock-face without numbers.

13 **circle** The image moves from the clock-face to the circle of the
universe created with perfect regularity ('even').

14 *blinds* because they hide the reality of eternity.

15 **this** this thought.

15–16 The end of time is the beginning of eternal life. The evening watch
(or religious vigil) is followed by Prime (the monastic office or service
appointed for the first hour of the day); but 'prime' can also mean the
most vigorous time of man's life.


# Peace

My soul, there is a country
    Far beyond the stars,
Where stands a wingèd sentry
    All skilful in the wars;
There above noise, and danger                     5
    Sweet peace sits crowned with smiles,
And one born in a manger
    Commands the beauteous files;
He is thy gracious friend,
    And (O my soul awake!)                        10
Did in pure love descend
    To die here for thy sake;
If thou canst get but thither,
    There grows the flower of peace,
The rose that cannot wither,                      15
    Thy fortress, and thy ease;

Leave then thy foolish ranges;
  For none can thee secure,
But one, who never changes,
  Thy God, thy life, thy cure.                                    20

**Peace**  the only one of Vaughan's poems regularly sung as a hymn.

8  **files**  ranks.

17  **ranges**  wanderings; or perhaps the ranks of the world who cannot
'secure' him.

# Quickness

False life! a foil and no more, when
            Wilt thou be gone?
Thou foul deception of all men
That would not have the true come on.

Thou art a moon-like toil; a blind                               5
            Self-posing state;
A dark contest of waves and wind;
A mere tempestuous debate.

Life is a fixed, discerning light,
            A knowing joy;                                       10
No chance, or fit: but ever bright,
And calm and full, yet doth not cloy.

'Tis such a blissful thing, that still
            Doth vivify,
And shine and smile, and hath the skill                         15
To please without Eternity.

Thou art a toilsome mole, or less,
            A moving mist;
But life is, what none can express,
*A quickness, which my God hath kissed.*                         20

**Quickness** Life.

1 **foil** a glittering deception as opposed to the 'light' of line 9 (metal foil looks attractive but hides whatever is underneath); perhaps also a contrast to true life.

4 **That . . . come on** that does not wish true life to thrive.

5 **moon-like** unreliable; the moon is not a 'fixed' light (line 9).
**toil** snare.

6 **self-posing** self-puzzling.

11 **fit** paroxysm, or sudden whim.

14 **vivify** animate.

16 **without Eternity** 'beyond Eternity', a hyperbolical way of saying eternally? or perhaps 'in this temporal world as opposed to in the eternal bliss of Heaven'?

17 **Thou** false life.
**toilsome** labouring; a punning echo of line 5. Moon, mist and underground mole are all deceptive.

20 'But God, who is rich in mercy, for his great love wherewith he loved us, Even when we were dead in sins, hath quickened us together with Christ' (Ephesians 2.4–5).

# Regeneration

A ward, and still in bonds, one day
    I stole abroad;
It was high-spring, and all the way
    *Primrosed*, and hung with shade;
      Yet, was it frost within,          5
        And surly winds
Blasted my infant buds, and sin
    Like clouds eclipsed my mind.

Stormed thus, I straight perceived my spring
    Mere stage, and show,          10
My walk a monstrous, mountained thing
    Rough-cast with rocks, and snow;
      And as a pilgrim's eye
        Far from relief,

Measures the melancholy sky            15
    Then drops, and rains for grief,

So sighed I upwards still; at last
    'Twixt steps, and falls
I reached the pinnacle, where placed
    I found a pair of scales;           20
    I took them up and laid
      In the one late pains;
The other smoke, and pleasures weighed
    But proved the heavier grains;

With that, some cried, *Away*; straight I      25
    Obeyed, and led
Full east, a fair, fresh field could spy;
    Some called it, *Jacob's bed*;
    A virgin-soil, which no
      Rude feet ere trod,            30
Where (since he stepped there) only go
    Prophets, and friends of God.

Here, I reposed; but scarce well set,
    A grove descried
Of stately height, whose branches met      35
    And mixed on every side;
    I entered, and once in
      (Amazed to see't)
Found all was changed, and a new spring
    Did all my senses greet;           40

The unthrift Sun shot vital gold
    A thousand pieces,
And heaven its azure did unfold
    Chequered with snowy fleeces;
    The air was all in spice           45
      And every bush
A garland wore; thus fed my eyes
    But all the ear lay hush.

Only a little fountain lent
    Some use for ears,           50

And on the dumb shades language spent,
 The music of her tears;
  I drew her near, and found
   The cistern full
Of divers stones, some bright and round,    55
 Others ill-shaped, and dull.

The first (pray mark) as quick as light
  Danced through the flood,
But, the last more heavy than the night
  Nailed to the centre stood;    60
   I wondered much, but tired
    At last with thought,
My restless eye that still desired
  As strange an object brought;

It was a bank of flowers, where I descried   65
  (Though 'twas mid-day)
Some fast asleep, others broad-eyed
  And taking in the ray;
   Here musing long, I heard
    A rushing wind    70
Which still increased, but whence it stirred
  Nor where I could not find;

I turned me round, and to each shade
  Dispatched an eye,
To see, if any leaf had made    75
  Least motion, or reply;
   But while I listening sought
    My mind to ease
By knowing, where 'twas, or where not,
  It whispered; *Where I please.*    80

  Lord, then said I, *On me one breath,*
  *And let me die before my death!*

Song of Solomon 4.16
*Arise O north, and come thou south-wind, and blow upon my*
*garden, that the spices thereof may flow out.*

**Regeneration** This was the opening poem of *Silex Scintillans* as it was first published in 1650. The closing quotation from the Song of Solomon (traditionally interpreted as 'The church prayeth to be made fit for [Christ's] presence') throws light on the imagery of the poem, as does this passage in which Jesus talks to Nicodemus of spiritual regeneration: 'Except a man be born of water and of the Spirit, he cannot enter into the kingdom of God . . . Marvel not that I said unto thee, Ye must be born again. The wind bloweth where it listeth [pleases], and thou hearest the sound thereof, but canst not tell whence it cometh, and whither it goeth: so is every one that is born of the Spirit' (John 3.5–8).

1  Vaughan is still a 'ward' of the world imprisoned by the 'bonds' of sin. He has not yet received the Spirit which will enable him to replace the guardianship of the world by the fatherhood of God: 'For as many as are led by the Spirit of God, they are the sons of God. For ye have not received the spirit of bondage again to fear; but ye have received the Spirit of adoption, whereby we cry, Abba, Father' (Romans 8.14–15).

2  **abroad**  outside.

5  **within**  in his own soul.

7  **infant buds**  compare line 2 of 'The Morning-Watch' (p140).

9  **stormed**  attacked by storms.
   **straight**  immediately.

10  **stage**  outward and transient show; compare 'Surely every man walketh in a vain show' (Psalm 39.6).

11–12  i.e. not spring at all.

20–4  The scales are an emblem of justice. Vaughan's recent sufferings count for less than his sinful pleasures, insubstantial ('smoke') though they are. Like Belshazzar he has been 'weighed in the balances and . . . found wanting' (Daniel 5.27).

27  **east**  suggests new life: the rising sun/Son and Easter.

28  *Jacob's bed*  The place where Jacob dreamed of a ladder set up to heaven and received God's blessing. Significantly he describes the place afterwards as 'the gate of heaven' (see Genesis 28).

30  **Rude**  irreverent.

34  **descried**  saw.

39  **a new spring**  not a 'Mere stage'.

41–2 The golden beams of the generous ('unthrift') sun are not just coins ('pieces') but living ('vital') gold, a spiritual elixir of life (see Herbert's 'The Elixir' on p85).

45 **spice** See closing quotation.

49 **fountain** suggests tears of repentance, water of baptism washing away sin (see quotation from John 3 in headnote), and Christ's grace: 'whosoever drinketh of the water that I shall give him shall never thirst; but the water that I shall give him shall be in him a well of water springing up into everlasting life' (John 4.14).

54 **cistern** pool surrounding the fountain.

55 **divers** various.

57 **mark** notice.
   **quick** living; St Peter describes Christ as the living corner stone and says that all Christians 'also, as lively stones, are built up a spiritual house . . . to offer up spiritual sacrifices, acceptable to God by Jesus Christ' (I Peter 2.5).

60 **centre** Hell was supposed to be at the centre of the earth.

64 **brought** to my notice.

68 The image of the stones, only some of which have responded to the life-giving influence of the water, is made more clear by that of the flowers, where again only some receive the 'ray' of 'vital gold' while others, like unregenerate souls, fail to respond to St Paul's words: 'now it is high time to awake out of sleep' (Romans 13.11).

70 **rushing wind** The coming of the Holy Spirit at Pentecost was accompanied by 'a sound from heaven as of a rushing mighty wind' (Acts 2.2). In the original Greek the same word is used for Spirit and wind. See also the passage from John in the headnote.

72 **Nor** I have accepted Daniel's emendation (see preface pvi) of 'No' to 'Nor' as following the scriptural reference and fitting in with line 79 more satisfactorily.

80 See headnote.

82 **let me die** to be 'dead to sin'; 'we are buried with [Christ] by baptism into death: that like as Christ was raised up from the dead . . . even so we also should walk in newness of life' (Romans 6.2 and 4).

# The Retreat

Happy those early days! when I
Shined in my Angel-infancy.
Before I understood this place
Appointed for my second race,
Or taught my soul to fancy aught                    5
But a white, celestial thought,
When yet I had not walked above
A mile, or two, from my first love,
And looking back (at that short space)
Could see a glimpse of his bright face;             10
When on some *gilded cloud*, or *flower*
My gazing soul would dwell an hour,
And in those weaker glories spy
Some shadows of eternity;
Before I taught my tongue to wound                  15
My conscience with a sinful sound,
Or had the black art to dispense
A several sin to every sense,
But felt through all this fleshly dress
Bright *shoots* of everlastingness.                 20
    O how I long to travel back
And tread again that ancient track!
That I might once more reach that plain,
Where first I left my glorious train,
From whence the enlightened spirit sees             25
That shady city of palm trees;
But (ah!) my soul with too much stay
Is drunk, and staggers in the way.
Some men a forward motion love,
But I by backward steps would move,                 30
And when this dust falls to the urn
In that state I came return.

2 **Angel-infancy** There is a hint here of the platonic concept of the pre-existence of the soul before birth, combined with Jesus' view of childish innocence: 'Except ye . . . become as little children, ye shall not enter into the kingdom of heaven' (Matthew 18.3).

4 **race** Life is 'the race that is set before us' (Hebrews 12.1).

12 **dwell** study lingeringly.

14 **shadows** faint images; Plato compares our sense experience in this
world with the shadows seen at the back of a cave by a man with a
fire behind him (*Republic* 7; see introduction, p4).

18 **several** separate.

19 **fleshly dress** the body.

20 Compare 'The Morning-Watch' line 2 (p140).

23–6 **that plain** Before Moses died on Mount Pisgah he saw the Promised
Land including 'the plain of the valley of Jericho, the city of the palm
trees' (Deuteronomy 34.3). Here the city becomes the 'new
Jerusalem' of heaven.'

24 **glorious train** the glory that followed him in his 'Angel-infancy'.

27 **too much stay** too long a stay in this world.

32 **that state** innocence of early childhood; see note on line 2.


# 'They are all gone into the world of light!'
## ¶

They are all gone into the world of light!
    And I alone sit lingering here;
Their very memory is fair and bright,
    And my sad thoughts doth clear.

It glows and glitters in my cloudy breast         5
    Like stars upon some gloomy grove,
Or those faint beams in which this hill is dressed,
    After the sun's remove.

I see them walking in an air of glory,
    Whose light doth trample on my days:       10
My days, which are at best but dull and hoary,
    Mere glimmering and decays.

O holy hope! and high humility,
    High as the Heavens above!
These are your walks, and you have showed them me     15
    To kindle my cold love,

Dear, beauteous death! the jewel of the just,
    Shining nowhere, but in the dark;
What mysteries do lie beyond thy dust;
    Could man outlook that mark!        20

He that hath found some fledged bird's nest, may know
    At first sight, if the bird be flown;
But what fair well, or grove he sings in now,
    That is to him unknown.

And yet, as Angels in some brighter dreams    25
    Call to the soul, when man doth sleep:
So some strange thoughts transcend our wonted themes,
    And into glory peep.

If a star were confined into a tomb
    Her captive flames must needs burn there;    30
But when the hand that locked her up, gives room,
    She'll shine through all the sphere.

O Father of eternal life, and all
    Created glories under thee!
Resume thy spirit from this world of thrall    35
    Into true liberty.

Either disperse these mists, which blot and fill
    My perspective (still) as they pass,
Or else remove me hence unto that hill,
    Where I shall need no glass.    40

See headnote to 'Joy of my life!' (p138).

1  **They** Vaughan's dead friends.

4  **clear** fill with light (the basic meaning of the word).

5  **It** the memory.

10  Vaughan's discontent with his 'dull' earthly days is intensified when he thinks of the radiant 'air of glory' of heaven.

11  **hoary** can mean mouldy; compare 'decays' in line 12.

15  **your walks** death's walks; the dead are like the stars above him 'walking in an air of glory'.

20  **outlook that mark** look beyond the death of the body ('dust').

21 **bird** a symbol of the soul; compare Marvell's 'The Garden', stanza 7 (p115).

23 **well** i.e. surroundings of a spring.

27 **transcend** rise above.
   **wonted** accustomed.

29–32 The soul confined in the body is like a star confined in a tomb. Death unlocks the soul from the body.

32 **sphere** vault of heaven.

35 **Resume . . . thrall** Take back to yourself the spirit that belongs to you (i.e. Vaughan's soul) from this world of slavery.

38 **perspective** telescope.

39 **that hill** heaven.

40 **glass** telescope.


# Unprofitableness

How rich, O Lord! how fresh thy visits are!
'Twas but just now my bleak leaves hopeless hung
     Sullied with dust and mud;
Each snarling blast shot through me, and did share
Their youth, and beauty; cold showers nipped, and wrung    5
     Their spiciness, and blood;
But since thou didst in one sweet glance survey
Their sad decays, I flourish, and once more
     Breathe all perfumes, and spice;
I smell a dew like *myrrh*, and all the day    10
Wear in my bosom a full Sun; such store
     Hath one beam from thy Eyes.
But, ah, my God! what fruit hast thou of this?
What one poor leaf did ever I yet fall
     To wait upon thy wreath?    15
Thus thou all day a thankless weed dost dress,
And when thou hast done, a stench, or fog is all
     The odour I bequeath.

Compare Herbert's 'The Flower' (p87).

4 **share** cut through (shear).

11 **store** abundance; a glance from God's eyes, like a ray of sun, bestows all these gifts.

14 **did ... fall** did I ever yet drop.

15 **To wait ... wreath** to be joined to your wreath (as a tribute of praise).

16 **dress** tend (a plant).

17–18 instead of a sweet scent.

# The Water-fall

With what deep murmurs through time's silent stealth
Doth thy transparent, cool and watery wealth
         Here flowing fall,
         And chide, and call,
As if his liquid, loose retinue stayed           5
Lingering, and were of this steep place afraid,
         The common pass
         Where, clear as glass,
         All must descend
         Not to an end:        10
But quickened by this deep and rocky grave,
Rise to a longer course more bright and brave.
Dear stream! dear bank, where often I
Have sat, and pleased my pensive eye,
Why, since each drop of thy quick store        15
Runs thither, whence it flowed before,
Should poor souls fear a shade or night,
Who came (sure) from a sea of light?
Or since those drops are all sent back
So sure to thee, that none doth lack,        20
Why should frail flesh doubt any more
That what God takes, he'll not restore?
O useful element and clear!
My sacred wash and cleanser here,

My first consigner unto those                                                    25
Fountains of life, where the Lamb goes!
What sublime truths, and wholesome themes,
Lodge in thy mystical, deep streams!
Such as dull man can never find
Unless that Spirit lead his mind,                                                30
Which first upon thy face did move,
And hatched all with his quickening love.
As this loud brook's incessant fall
In streaming rings restagnates all,
Which reach by course the bank, and then                                         35
Are no more seen, just so pass men.
O my invisible estate,
My glorious liberty, still late!
Thou art the channel my soul seeks,
Not this with cataracts and creeks.                                              40

1    **time's silent stealth** As the flow of the river brings it to the waterfall
     so the quiet passing of time brings man to physical death.

4–6  The sound of the waterfall is like a voice rebuking ('chiding') the
     river for its fear.

5    **retinue** stressed on second syllable; followers.

7    **common** to all; neither waterfall nor death can be escaped.

11   **quickened** made to move faster; brought to life.

12   **brave** attractive.

15   **quick** living.

16   **Runs thither . . . before** goes to the place from which it previously
     came; i.e., from sea to cloud, to rain, to river, and now back to sea
     again.

7–18 **Should . . . light** Why should souls which are like drops of water
     drawn up from heaven's 'sea of light' fear death? (since like water
     they will return to their starting point).

20   **none doth lack** not one is missing.

23–4 the water of baptism which washes away sin.

25–6 Baptism is the first stage in 'consigning' or passing Vaughan on to
     heaven where 'the Lamb [Christ] . . . shall lead them unto living
     fountains of waters' (Revelation 7.17).

30–32 The opening act of Creation by God's Spirit is described thus: 'And the Spirit of God moved upon the face of the waters' (Genesis 1.2).

34 **restagnates** makes still again (but no idea of corruption).

35–6 As the water moves from activity to stillness so man moves from life to death. To be 'no more seen' implies death: 'O spare me a little, that I may recover my strength: before I go hence, and be no more seen' (Psalm 39.15).

38 **glorious liberty** a quotation from St Paul writing of man's hope for full sonship of God when the body is set free by the resurrection: 'the creature itself also shall be delivered from the bondage of corruption into the glorious liberty of the children of God' (Romans 8.21).

39–40 Vaughan wishes to move from the earthly symbol to the heavenly reality.

# The World (1)

I saw Eternity the other night
Like a great *Ring* of pure and endless light,
    All calm, as it was bright,
And round beneath it, Time in hours, days, years
      Driven by the spheres       5
Like a vast shadow moved, in which the world
    And all her train were hurled;
The doting lover in his quaintest strain
      Did there complain;
Near him, his lute, his fancy, and his flights,       10
      Wit's sour delights,
With gloves, and knots, the silly snares of pleasure
      Yet his dear treasure,
All scattered lay, while he his eyes did pour
      Upon a flower.       15

The darksome states-man hung with weights and woe
Like a thick midnight-fog moved there so slow
    He did nor stay, nor go;
Condemning thoughts (like sad eclipses) scowl
      Upon his soul,       20

And clouds of crying witnesses without
    Pursued him with one shout.
Yet digged the mole, and lest his ways be found
    Worked under ground,
Where he did clutch his prey, but one did see    25
    That policy;
Churches and altars fed him; perjuries
    Were gnats and flies;
It rained about him blood and tears, but he
    Drank them as free.    30

The fearful miser on a heap of rust
Sat pining all his life there, did scarce trust
    His own hands with the dust,
Yet would not place one piece above, but lives
    In fear of thieves.    35
Thousands there were as frantic as himself
    And hugged each one his pelf;
The down-right epicure placed heaven in sense
    And scorned pretence,
While others slipped into a wide excess    40
    Said little less;
The weaker sort slight, trivial wares enslave,
    Who think them brave;
And poor, despisèd truth sat counting by
    Their victory.    45

Yet some, who all this while did weep and sing,
And sing, and weep, soared up into the *Ring*,
    But most would use no wing.
O fools (said I) thus to prefer dark night
    Before true light,    50
To live in grots, and caves, and hate the day
    Because it shows the way,
The way which from this dead and dark abode
    Leads up to God,
A way where you might tread the Sun, and be    55
    More bright than he.

But as I did their madness so discuss
    One whispered thus,
*This ring the bride-groom did for none provide*
    *But for his bride.*         60

I John 2.16–17
*All that is in the world, the lust of the flesh, the lust of the*
*eyes, and the pride of life, is not of the father but is of the*
*world.*
    *And the world passeth away, and the lusts thereof, but he*
*that doth the will of God abideth for ever.*

**The World** all that is worldly (as opposed to spiritual) and cannot escape space and time to reach the eternity of heaven; see the closing quotation from I John.

1–7 Vaughan adapts Plato's description in *Timaeus* of Time as a moving image of the ring of Eternity, made up of the circling spheres of the physical universe.

7 **train** literally followers, but here inhabitants.
**hurled** whirled round.

8 **quaintest** most full of elaborate figures of speech.

9 **complain** lament his unhappy love.

10 **flights** of poetic fancy, or of whimsical love.

12 **knots** like the gloves, the love-knots are mementoes of worldly love, but they suggest the danger of being trapped in the 'snares of pleasure'.

13 **Yet** but nevertheless.

14 **pour** study closely, or weep; the lover has no eyes for Eternity.

23 **mole** blind, secretive and undermining things.

25 **one** God.

26 **policy** political cunning.

28 **gnats and flies** i.e. insignificant.

31–5 'Lay not up for yourselves treasures upon earth, where moth and rust doth corrupt, and where thieves break through and steal: But lay up for yourselves treasures in heaven, where neither moth nor rust doth corrupt, and where thieves do not break through nor steal: For where your treasure is, there will your heart be also' (Matthew 6.19–21).

34 **place one piece above** invest one coin in heaven.

37 **pelf** ill-gotten gains.

38 **The down-right . . . sense** The plain-spoken glutton found his heaven in sensual gratification.

42-3 **The weaker . . . brave** The paltry, frivolous goods of this world enslave the weaker characters who think them splendid.

44 **counting** reckoning the cost.

49-56 In Plato's parable of the cave (see introduction p4 and note to line 14 of 'The Retreat' p151) the man who has only seen shadows resists any attempt to take him outside into the sunlight. In Christian terms the sun is God himself.

59 The ring of eternity has become the wedding ring for the marriage of the Lamb (Christ) and his bride the Church (see Revelation 19).


# The Wreath

Since I in storms used most to be
    And seldom yielded flowers,
How shall I get a wreath for thee
    From those rude, barren hours?

The softer dressings of the spring,                   5
    Or summer's later store
I will not for thy temples bring,
    Which *thorns*, not *roses* wore.

But a twined wreath of *grief* and *praise*,
Praise soiled with tears, and tears again          10
Shining with joy, like dewy days,
This day I bring for all thy pain,
Thy causeless pain! and, sad as death,
Which sadness breeds in the most vain,
(O not in vain!) now beg thy breath;          15
Thy quickening breath, which gladly bears
Through saddest clouds to that glad place,
Where cloudless choirs sing without tears,
Sing thy just praise, and see thy face.

**The Wreath** Both subject matter and style are derived from Herbert's poem of this title (p101).

3 **thee** Christ, who wore a crown of thorns (line 8).

14 **vain** those who are caught up in vain follies.

16 **breath** of life; the Holy Spirit; see note to line 70 of 'Regeneration' (p149).

# Other Poems

## Christopher Marlowe 1564–1593
## Ovid's Elegies, Book I, 13

*Ad auroram, ne properet*

Now o'er the sea from her old love comes she
That draws the day from heaven's cold axle-tree.
Aurora, whither slidest thou? down again,
And birds for Memnon yearly shall be slain.
Now in her tender arms I sweetly bide,                                      5
If ever, now well lies she by my side.
The air is cold, and sleep is sweetest now,
And birds send forth shrill notes from every bough:
Whither runn'st thou, that men and women love not?
Hold in thy rosy horses that they move not.                                10
Ere thou rise, stars teach seamen where to sail,
But when thou comest, they of their courses fail.
Poor travellers, though tired, rise at thy sight,
And soldiers make them ready to the fight.
The painful hind by thee to field is sent,                                 15
Slow oxen early in the yoke are pent.
Thou cozen'st boys of sleep, and dost betray them
To pedants that with cruel lashes pay them.
Thou mak'st the surety to the lawyer run,
That with one word hath nigh himself undone.                               20
The lawyer and the client hate thy view,
Both whom thou raisest up to toil anew.
By thy means women of their rest are barred,
Thou set'st their labouring hands to spin and card.
All could I bear; but that the wench should rise                           25

Who can endure, save him with whom none lies?
How oft wished I night would not give thee place,
Nor morning stars shun thy uprising face.
How oft that either wind would break thy coach,
Or steeds might fall, forced with thick clouds' approach.    30
Whither goest thou, hateful nymph? Memnon the elf
Received his coal-black colour from thyself.
Say that thy love with Cephalus were not known,
Then thinkest thou thy loose life is not shown?
Would Tithon might but talk of thee awhile,    35
Not one in heaven should be more base and vile.
Thou leav'st his bed because he's faint through age,
And early mount'st thy hateful carriage;
But held'st thou in thine arms some Cephalus,
Then wouldst thou cry, 'Stay night, and run not thus.'    40
Dost punish me, because years make him wane?
I did not bid thee wed an ancient swain.
The moon sleeps with Endymion every day;
Thou art as fair as she, then kiss and play.
Jove, that thou shouldst not haste but wait his leisure,    45
Made two nights one to finish up his pleasure.
I chid no more; she blushed, and therefore heard me,
Yet lingered not the day, but morning scared me.

Ovid's love elegies are the best-known examples of a type of poetry
that influenced poets such as Donne not only in their choice of form
(Donne's own elegies), but also in their subject matter (e.g. 'The Sun
Rising'). Here the poet is enjoying the pleasures of the night and the
purpose of the poem is made clear in its Latin title: 'To Aurora
(goddess of dawn) not to hurry'.

1  **old love** Aurora married a mortal, Tithon (lines 35–8), who was
   granted eternal life but not eternal youth.

2  **axle-tree** used both to describe the rotation of the universe and more
   loosely to mean the sky.

3–4  **down again . . . slain** If you go down again birds will be sacrificed
   each year for Memnon. Memnon was Aurora's son, killed by
   Achilles at Troy but then granted immortality. A flock of birds
   emerged from his funeral pyre and fought over it until half of them

were consumed in the flames as a sacrifice to him. Supposedly the birds returned to the tomb every year.

9 **that** so that.

10 **rosy horses** Dawn is imagined crossing the sky in a chariot; rosy is the traditional adjective used for dawn.

14 **them** themselves.

15 **hind** farm labourer.

16 **pent** imprisoned.

17 **cozen'st** cheat.

18 **pedants** schoolmasters.

19 **surety** one who has guaranteed the payment of debt or appearance in court of another.

24 **card** comb out wool prior to spinning.

29 **coach** Dawn's chariot.

30 **forced** overpowered.

33 **Cephalus** also loved by Aurora.

34 **loose** immoral.

35 **Would . . . awhile** If Tithon were only to talk about you for a while . . .

39 **some Cephalus** i.e. a young man.

40 With terrible irony Marlowe was to put the original Latin ('O *lente, lente currite, noctis equi*', 'Run slowly, slowly, horses of the night') into the mouth of Faust as the hour of his final damnation approached.

41 **him wane** Tithon grow old.

43 **Diana** goddess of the moon, loved Endymion.

45–6 The intervening day was turned to night as well when Jove slept with Alcmena and Hercules was conceived.

# Ben Jonson 1573–1637
## To Celia

Come my *Celia*, let us prove,
While we may, the sports of love;
Time will not be ours, for ever:
He, at length, our good will sever.
Spend not then his gifts in vain.                    5
Suns, that set, may rise again:
But if once we lose this light,
'Tis, with us, perpetual night.
Why should we defer our joys?
Fame, and rumour are but toys.                        10
Cannot we delude the eyes
Of a few poor household spies?
Or his easier ears beguile,
So removèd by our wile?
'Tis no sin, love's fruit to steal,                  15
But the sweet theft to reveal:
To be taken, to be seen,
These have crimes accounted been.

This song, imitating the Latin poet Catullus (*Carmina V*), appears in
Jonson's *Volpone*. Volpone sings it while attempting to seduce the
virtuous wife, Celia. Its theme of *carpe diem* (seize the day) is often
repeated (see especially Marvell's 'To His Coy Mistress', p103).

13 **his** the husband's.

# Richard Lovelace 1618–58
## Carmina LXXII of Catullus

That me alone you loved, you once did say,
Nor should I to the King of gods give way;
Then I loved thee not as a common dear,
But as a Father doth his children cheer;
Now thee I know, more bitterly I smart,               5
Yet thou to me more light and cheaper art.

What power is this? that such a wrong should press
Me to love more, yet wish thee well much less.

Parallels of both the subject matter and the witty paradox of the
conclusion of this song by Catullus can be found in metaphysical
poetry.

3 **common dear**  woman available to all.

# Sir Richard Fanshawe 1608–66
# Martial's Epigrams, Book X, 47

*A Happy Life*

The things that make a life to please
(Sweetest Martial) they are these:
Estate inherited, not got:
A thankful field, hearth always hot:
City seldom, lawsuits never:                                   5
Equal friends agreeing ever:
Health of body, peace of mind:
Sleeps that till the morning bind:
Wise simplicity, plain fare:
Not drunken nights, yet loosed from care:                      10
A sober, not a sullen spouse:
Clean strength, not such as his that ploughs:
Wish only what thou art, to be;
Death neither wish, nor fear to see.

Classical epigrams were short poems marked by compression and
wit. They were frequently translated and imitated (see examples by
Donne) and although seldom of great value in themselves their terse
wit did influence metaphysical poetry. This translation of Martial
introduces the ideal of rural virtue and retirement which appealed so
much to Marvell.

3 **got**  acquired (perhaps by dubious means).
4 **thankful**  giving a good yield.
13 **Wish only . . . be**  Be satisfied with your station in life.

# Joseph Hall 1574–1656
## Virgidemiarum Book I, Satire 7

Great is the folly of a feeble brain,
O'er-ruled with love, and tyrannous disdain:
For love, however in the basest breast
It breeds high thoughts that feed the fancy best,
Yet is he blind, and leads poor fools awry,                    5
While they hang gazing on their mistress' eye.
The love-sick poet, whose importune prayer
Repulsèd is with resolute despair,
Hopeth to conquer his disdainful dame,
With public plaints of his conceivèd flame.                   10
Then pours he forth in patchèd sonettings
His love, his lust, and loathsome flatterings:
As though the staring world hanged on his sleeve,
When once he smiles, to laugh: and when he sighs, to grieve.
Careth the world, thou love, thou live, or die?               15
Careth the world, how fair thy fair one be?
Fond wit-old, that would'st load thy wit-less head
With timely horns, before thy bridal bed.
Then can he term his dirty ill-faced bride
Lady and Queen, and virgin deified:                           20
Be she all sooty-black, or berry-brown,
She's white as morrow's milk, or flakes new blown.
And though she be some dunghill drudge at home,
Yet can he her resign some refuse room
Amidst the well-known stars: or if not there,                 25
Sure will he saint her in his calendar.

**Virgidemiarum** Joseph Hall's six books 'of sound floggings'
('virgidemiarum') were, so he claimed, the first satires in English and
were published in 1597 and 1598. This example is similar to Donne's
not only in its direct, blunt language, but also in its cynicism about
love and its scorn of Petrarchan love imagery (see introduction, p6).

3 **however** although.
5 **blind** Cupid is blind.
  **awry** astray.

7 **importune** irritatingly persistent.

8 **despair** strong discouragement? (as in the *Oxford English Dictionary*, variant 2: to cast into despair), but since the original spelling is 'dispayre' a pun is perhaps intended with the meaning of separation.

10 **plaints** lamentations.
**conceivèd flame** the passionate affection that originated in his mind.

11 **patchèd sonettings** poorly versified and derivative attempts at love songs; both words express contempt.

13 **hanged on his sleeve** depended on him.

17 **Fond wit-old** doting cuckold; a wit-old or wittol is a man who knows of, and is complaisant about, his wife's infidelity. The word can also mean a fool and leads naturally by sound and meaning to 'wit-less'.

18 **timely horns** early horns; cuckolds were supposed to grow horns and by telling everyone that the woman does not love him even before marriage the foolish lover acquires his horns in record time.

20 **deified** made a goddess.

22 **morrow's** morning's.
**flakes** snow.

23 **drudge** a menial servant.

24-5 **Yet can . . . stars** Yet he can allocate her some corner in the skies amongst the well known stars where rubbish can be dumped; a sneering reference to the many classical legends in which beautiful women were changed into stars.

# Ben Jonson 1573–1637
## My Picture Left in Scotland

> I now think, Love is rather deaf, than blind,
>> For else it could not be,
>>> That she,
> Whom I adore so much, should so slight me,
>> And cast my love behind:          5

I'm sure my language to her, was as sweet,
  And every close did meet
  In sentence, of as subtle feet,
   As hath the youngest He,
  That sits in shadow of *Apollo's* tree.   10
Oh, but my conscious fears,
  That fly my thoughts between,
  Tell me that she hath seen
  My hundreds of grey hairs,
  Told seven and forty years.   15
Read so much waist, as she cannot embrace
  My mountain belly, and my rocky face,
And all these through her eyes, have stopped her ears.

Ben Jonson was an exact contemporary of Donne and although his
poetry is not metaphysical it is similar in its personal tone, plain
language and metrical variety.

7–8   **And every . . . feet** the conclusion (musical and poetical) of every
  phrase coincided with a witty aphorism, the metre was as subtle . . .

10   Apollo was the god of poetic inspiration.

16   **waist** a pun on 'waste'.


# Richard Lovelace 1618–58
# The Scrutiny

Why should you swear I am forsworn,
  Since thine I vowed to be?
Lady it is already morn,
  And 'twas last night I swore to thee
That fond impossibility.   5

Have I not loved thee much and long,
  A tedious twelve hours' space?
I must all other beauties wrong,
  And rob thee of a new embrace;
Could I still dote upon thy face.   10

Not, but all joy in thy brown hair,
	By others may be found;
But I must search the black and fair
	Like skilful mineralists that sound
For treasure in unploughed-up ground.	15

Then, if when I have loved my round,
	Thou prov'st the pleasant she;
With spoils of meaner beauties crowned,
	I laden will return to thee,
Ev'n sated with variety.	20

In this poem Lovelace continues the cynically flippant tradition of
anti-Petrarchan poems like Donne's 'Woman's Constancy' (p54).

5 **fond** doting, and foolish.

11–12 **Not . . . found** Not that others aren't welcome to find every delight
in thy brown hair . . .

14 **sound** mine.

16 **my round** of the other beauties.

20 **Ev'n sated** sated as I shall be.

# Richard Lovelace 1618–58
# To Lucasta, Going Beyond the Seas

If to be absent were to be
	Away from thee;
	Or that when I am gone,
	You or I were alone;
Then my *Lucasta* might I crave	5
Pity from blustering wind, or swallowing wave.

But I'll not sigh one blast or gale
	To swell my sail,
	Or pay a tear to swage
	The foaming blue God's rage;	10
For whether he will let me pass
Or no, I'm still as happy as I was.

Though seas and land be 'twixt us both,
　　　Our faith and troth,
　　　　Like separated souls,                    15
　　　　All time and space controls:
Above the highest sphere we meet
Unseen, unknown, and greet as angels greet.

So then we do anticipate
　　　Our after-fate,                            20
　　　　And are alive in the skies
　　　　If thus our lips and eyes
Can speak like spirits unconfined
In Heaven, their earthy bodies left behind.

Compare to 'A Valediction: forbidding Mourning' (p51) and 'To
Amoret, of the Difference 'Twixt Him, and Other Lovers' (p133).

 9 **swage** assuage.
10 **blue God** Neptune.
13 **be 'twixt** be between.
14 **troth** mutually exchanged faith.
17 **above the highest sphere** beyond time and space; in heaven.
23 **unconfined** by bodies.

# Thomas Stanley 1625–78
# The Divorce

Dear, back my wounded heart restore,
　　And turn away thy powerful eyes,
Flatter my willing soul no more,
　　Love must not hope what Fate denies.

Take, take away thy smiles and kisses,          5
　　Thy love wounds deeper than disdain,
For he that sees the Heaven he misses,
　　Sustains two Hells, of loss and pain.

Shouldst thou some other's suit prefer,
   I might return thy scorn to thee,          10
And learn apostasy of her
   Who taught me first idolatry.

Or in thy unrelenting breast
   Should I disdain or coyness move,
He by thy hate might be released,          15
   Who now is prisoner to thy love.

Since then unkind Fate will divorce
   Those whom affection long united,
Be thou as cruel as this force,
   And I in death shall be delighted.        20

Thus whilst so many suppliants woo
   And beg they may thy pity prove,
I only for thy scorn do sue;
   'Tis charity here not to love.

11  **apostasy**  abandoning of religious faith (his love of the woman whom he 'idolises').

14  **coyness**  reluctance to respond to his advances.
    **move**  arouse.

20  Her rejection of him would kill him, but he would be 'delighted' because it would end his suffering.

22  **prove**  have experience of.

24  The paradox repeats the idea of line 20.

# William Habington 1605–54
## To Castara: the reward of innocent love

We saw and wooed each others' eyes,
   My soul contracted then with thine
And both burnt in one sacrifice
   By which our marriage grew divine.

Let wilder youth, whose soul is sense,                    5
    Profane the temple of delight
And purchase endless penitence
    With the stolen pleasure of one night.

Time's ever ours while we despise
    The sensual idol of our clay,                         10
For though the sun doth set and rise,
    We 'joy one everlasting day

Whose light no jealous clouds obscure
    While each of us shine innocent;
The troubled stream is still impure;                      15
    With virtue flies away content.

And though opinions often err,
    We'll court the modest smile of fame;
For sin's black danger circles her
    Who hath infection in her name.                       20

Thus when to one dark silent room
    Death shall our loving coffins thrust,
Fame will build columns on our tomb
    And add a perfume to our dust.

**Castara**  the chaste woman; the poem is a celebration of platonic
love.

2  **contracted**  made a contract.

5  This echoes 'A Valediction: forbidding Mourning' (p51).

10  **clay**  bodies.

15  **still**  always.

16  **With virtue . . . content**  When virtue is lost, so is happiness.

# Sir Philip Sidney 1554–86
## Psalm 13

How long, O Lord, shall I forgotten be?
    What? ever?
How long wilt Thou Thy hidden face from me
    Dissever?

How long shall I consult with careful sprite        5
    In anguish?
How long shall I with foes' triumphant might
    Thus languish?

Behold me, Lord, let to Thy hearing creep
    My crying:        10
Nay give me eyes, and light, lest that I sleep
    In dying;

Lest my foe brag, that in my ruin he
    Prevailèd,
And at my fall they joy that, troublous, me        15
    Assailèd.

No, no, I trust on Thee, and joy in Thy
    Great pity.
Still therefore of Thy graces shall be my
    Song's ditty.        20

Both the theme of the Psalmist's spiritual desolation and the verse form of this translation with its distinctive use of short lines may be presumed to have influenced Herbert in such poems as 'Denial' (p82).

4 **Dissever** separate.

5 **careful** i.e. full of cares.

# Robert Southwell 1561–95
## The Burning Babe

As I in hoary winter's night stood shivering in the snow,
Surprised I was with sudden heat, which made my heart to
  glow;
And lifting up a fearful eye, to view what fire was near,
A pretty Babe all burning bright did in the air appear;
Who scorchèd with excessive heat, such floods of tears did
  shed,          5
As though his floods should quench his flames, which with his
  tears were bred:
Alas (quoth he) but newly born, in fiery heats I fry,
Yet none approach to warm their hearts or feel my fire, but I;
My faultless breast the furnace is, the fuel wounding thorns:
Love is the fire, and sighs the smoke, the ashes, shames and
  scorns;         10
The fuel Justice layeth on, and Mercy blows the coals;
The metal in this furnace wrought, are men's defilèd souls:
For which, as now on fire I am to work them to their good,
So will I melt into a bath, to wash them in my blood.
With this he vanished out of sight, and swiftly shrunk away, 15
And straight I callèd unto mind, that it was Christmas day.

This poem provides an early example of a conceit making use of
Christian imagery. It also shows the meditational practice of using
the imagination as a prelude and stimulus to devotion. Compare 'At
the round earth's imagined corners' (p67).

9 **faultless** Christ was the only perfect man.
  **thorns** Christ's crown of thorns on the cross.

11 Justice demands that the penalty for sin should be paid, but Christ in
  his mercy dies for man himself.

12 **wrought** shaped; men's souls are not only purified in the fire but also
  'worked . . . to their good'.

16 **straight** immediately.

# Richard Crashaw 1612–49
## Easter Day

Rise, heir of fresh eternity,
  From thy virgin tomb!
Rise, mighty Man of wonders, and thy world with thee!
  Thy tomb, the universal east,
    Nature's new womb;      5
Thy tomb fair immortality's perfumèd nest.

Of all the glories make noon gay,
  This is the morn;
This rock buds forth the fountain of the streams of day;
  In joy's white annals lives this hour   10
    When life was born:
No cloud scowl on his radiant lids, no tempest lower.

Life, by this light's nativity,
  All creatures have;
Death only by this day's just doom is forced to die;  15
  Nor is death forced: for may he lie
    Throned in thy grave,
Death will on this condition be content to die.

 4 **universal east** Christ's resurrection makes it possible for all to rise
  just as the sun does. Compare last two stanzas of Herbert's 'Easter'
  (p83).
 9 **rock** the sepulchre in which Christ was buried, but also the rock
  which Moses struck to give water in the desert (Numbers 20).
  **buds** suggests spring and new life.
15 **doom** judgement.
18 See the conclusion of *Divine Meditations* 10 (p68).

# Richard Crashaw 1612–49
## On Mary Magdalene

Luke 7
*She began to wash his feet with tears,*
*and wipe them with the hairs of her head*

Her eyes' flood licks his feet's fair stain,
Her hair's flame licks up that again;
This flame thus quenched hath brighter beams,
This flood thus stainèd, fairer streams.

See note on Herbert's 'Mary Magdalene' (p93).

2   **hair's flame**   by tradition Mary's hair was red.

# Thomas Traherne 1637/8–74
## On News

     News from a foreign country came
As if my treasure and my wealth lay there;
    So much it did my heart inflame,
'Twas wont to call my Soul into mine ear;
        Which thither went to meet         5
          The approaching sweet,
        And on the threshold stood
To entertain the Unknown Good.
        It hovered there
         As if 'twould leave mine ear,      10
    And was so eager to embrace
The joyful tidings as they came,
    'Twould almost leave its dwelling-place
        To entertain the same.

     As if the tidings were the things,     15
My very joys themselves, my foreign treasure,
    Or else did bear them on their wings,

With so much joy they came, with so much pleasure.
    My Soul stood at the gate
       To recreate               20
    Itself with bliss, and to
Be pleased with speed. A fuller view
    It fain would take,
    Yet journeys back would make
Unto my heart; as if 'twould fain       25
Go out to meet, yet stay within
To fit a place to entertain,
    And bring the tidings in.

    What sacred instinct did inspire
My soul in childhood with a hope so strong?    30
    What secret force moved my desire
To expect my joys beyond the seas, so young?
      Felicity I knew
        Was out of view;
      And being here alone,      35
I saw that happiness was gone
      From me! For this
    I thirsted absent bliss,
And thought that sure beyond the seas,
Or else in something near at hand      40
(I knew not yet, since nought did please
    I knew) my Bliss did stand.

    But little did the infant dream
That all the treasures of the world were by:
    And that himself was so the cream      45
And crown of all which round about did lie.
      Yet thus it was: the Gem,
        The Diadem,
      The Ring enclosing all
    That stood upon this earthy ball,     50
      The heavenly Eye,
    Much wider than the sky,
Wherein they all included were,
The glorious Soul, that was the King
Made to possess them, did appear      55
    A small and little thing!

Traherne shares with Vaughan a belief in the innocence and perceptiveness of 'angel-infancy' ('The Retreat' p150). See also Marvell's 'The Picture of little T. C.' (p112). The title and opening of the poem are derived from Proverbs 25.25: 'As cold waters to a thirsty soul, So is good news from a far country.'

20 **recreate** refresh.

23 **It fain would** it wished to.

41–2 **I knew . . . I knew** I did not yet know where, since I *did* know that nothing I had experienced so far had pleased me.

49 **The Ring** a sphere of soul which encompasses the universe; the soul of the innocent child comes from God and has the divine imprint. (Original sin appears to play no part in Traherne's thinking.) The next poem presents the idea of an interior world in another way.


# Thomas Traherne 1637/8–74
# Dreams

'Tis strange! I saw the skies,
I saw the hills before mine eyes,
    The sparrow fly,
The lands that did about me lie,
The real sun, that heavenly eye.         5
Can closed eyes even in the darkest night
See through their lids and be informed with sight?

    The people were to me
As true as those by day I see;
    As true the air;         10
The earth as sweet, as fresh, as fair
As that which did by day repair
Unto my waking sense: can all the sky,
Can all the world, within my brain-pan lie?

    What sacred secret's this         15
Which seems to intimate my bliss?
    What is there in

The narrow confines of my skin
That is alive and feels within
When I am dead? Can magnitude possess                    20
An active memory, yet not be less?

      May all that I can see,
Awake, by night, within me be?
      My childhood knew
No difference, but all was true,                          25
    As real all as what I view;
The world itself was there: 'twas wondrous strange
That heaven and earth should so their place exchange.

     Till that which vulgar sense
Doth falsely call experience                              30
      Distinguished things,
The ribands and the gaudy wings
Of birds, the virtues and the sins,
That represented were in dreams by night
As really my senses did delight,                          35

    Or grieve, as those I saw
By day; things terrible did awe
      My soul with fear;
The apparitions seemed as near
As things could be, and things they were:                 40
Yet were they all by fancy in me wrought
And all their being founded in a thought.

    O what a thing is thought!
Which seems a dream, yea, seemeth nought,
     Yet doth the mind                             45
   Affect as much as what we find
   Most near and true. Sure, men are blind
And can't the forcible reality
Of things that secret are within them see.

    Thought! Surely thoughts are true?            50
They please as much as things can do –
     Nay, things are dead

And in themselves are severèd
From souls, nor can they fill the head
Without our thoughts. Thoughts are the real things          55
From whence all joy, from whence all sorrow springs.

Compare Marvell's 'The Garden' for a withdrawal into an internal
world of the mind (p114).

29–31  **Till that . . . things** Until that which commonly accepted wisdom
falsely calls experience enabled me to distinguish between dream and
waking . . . Traherne feels that 'experience' merely destroys the
child's intuition.

32  **ribands** ornamental ribbons.

35  **really** three syllables.

41  **wrought** created.


# Ralph Knevet 1600–71/2
# The Vote

The helmet now an hive for bees becomes
And hilts of swords may serve for spiders' looms;
    Sharp pikes may make
    Teeth for a rake
And the keen blade, the arch-enemy of life,                  5
Shall be degraded to a pruning-knife;
    The rustic spade,
    Which first was made
For honest agriculture, shall retake
Its primitive employment and forsake                         10
    The rampires steep
    And trenches deep.
Tame conies in our brazen guns shall breed
Or gentle doves their young ones there shall feed;
    In musket barrels                                    15
    Mice shall raise quarrels
For their quarters. The ventriloquious drum,

Like lawyers in vacation, shall be dumb.
    Now all recruits
    But those of fruits                    20
Shall be forgot; and the unarmed soldier
Shall only boast of what he did whilere,
    In chimney's ends
    Among his friends.

If good effects shall happy signs ensue,        25
I shall rejoice, and my prediction's true.

The starting point of this poem is an emblem which appears in
Geoffrey Whitney's *A Choice of Emblems* (1585). Beneath a picture
of a helmet surrounded by bees the verse reads:

The helmet strong, that did the head defend,
Behold, for hive, the bees in quiet served:
And when that wars, with bloody blows, had end,
They honey wrought, where soldier was preserved:
    Which doth declare, the blessed fruits of peace,
    How sweet she is, when mortal wars do cease.

3–6  Compare 'They shall beat their swords into plowshares, and their
     spears into pruning hooks: nation shall not lift up sword against
     nation, neither shall they learn war any more' (Isaiah 2.4).

11  **rampires** ramparts.

13  **conies** rabbits.

22  **whilere** formerly.

25  **ensue** follow as a consequence.

# Index of First Lines